DEMOCRATIC WEALTH STEWARDSHIP

DEMOCRATIC WEALTH STEWARDSHIP

Governing Concentrated Wealth for the Public Good

BY

NANCY S. LIND
Illinois State University, USA

emerald PUBLISHING

United Kingdom – North America – Japan – India
Malaysia – China

Emerald Publishing Limited
Emerald Publishing, Floor 5, Northspring, 21-23 Wellington Street, Leeds LS1 4DL

First edition 2026

British Library Cataloguing in Publication Data
A catalogue record for this book is available from the British Library

ISBN: 978-1-83742-255-5 (Print)
ISBN: 978-1-83742-254-8 (Online)
ISBN: 978-1-83742-256-2 (Epub)

Printed and bound by CPI Group (UK) Ltd, Croydon, CR0 4YY

INVESTOR IN PEOPLE

CONTENTS

INTRODUCTION: DEMOCRACY UNDER SIEGE AND THE CASE FOR WEALTH STEWARDSHIP

ABSTRACT

This book addresses one of the most pressing challenges facing twenty-first-century democracies: how to govern extreme wealth concentration that simultaneously threatens democratic institutions and provides resources for addressing urgent public challenges. Drawing on political science, economics, legal theory and empirical evidence from global case studies, the author develops the Democratic Wealth Stewardship Framework – a comprehensive governance approach reconceptualising concentrated wealth as power requiring democratic accountability rather than absolute private property rights. The framework rests on five interconnected principles: reframing property rights as stewardship obligations, ensuring meaningful citizen participation in wealth governance, embedding intergenerational justice in decision-making, balancing democratic deliberation with governance effectiveness, and preventing wealth's weaponisation for authoritarian purposes. These principles address critical democratic deficits in current wealth governance while preserving innovation capacity and legitimate wealth accumulation. The analysis demonstrates how extreme wealth concentration enables authoritarian threats through information control, policy capture, trust erosion and parallel governance structures that bypass democratic accountability. It examines the innovation-democracy tension, showing how crisis convergence – climate emergency, biodiversity collapse, AI disruption, inequality and democratic erosion – creates pressure for rapid responses that democratic processes struggle to provide, yet authoritarian alternatives prove illusory and dangerous. The book presents concrete policy mechanisms spanning pre-distribution (preventing extreme concentration through progressive taxation, inheritance limits, antitrust enforcement) and post-distribution (governing wealth deployment through foundation oversight, participatory grantmaking, transparency requirements). It analyses international examples of participatory democracy – from Porto Alegre's participatory budgeting to Taiwan's digital democracy – demonstrating feasible governance innovations. Implementation strategies address political economy challenges, coalition-building across diverse constituencies and mechanisms for sustaining reforms against elite resistance. Throughout, the framework centres on racial and class justice, recognising how wealth concentration reflects and reinforces historical injustices rooted in colonialism, slavery and ongoing extraction. The analysis examines how philanthropic resource flows perpetuate racial inequalities and how democratic wealth governance must institutionalise equity accountability as obligation rather than voluntary enlightenment. This work contributes to scholarship on democratic theory, economic inequality and institutional design by integrating insights across disciplines to develop actionable governance mechanisms. It speaks to policymakers, advocates, scholars and citizens concerned with preserving democratic self-governance while addressing civilisation-scale challenges. The framework offers neither utopian idealism nor technocratic quick fixes, but rather institutionally grounded democratic mechanisms responsive to contemporary political possibilities and constraints.

Keywords: Democratic wealth stewardship; concentrated wealth governance; participatory democracy; economic inequality; racial wealth justice; foundation accountability

On 6 January 2021, insurrectionists stormed the United States Capitol. As cameras captured violence in the heart of American democracy, a less visible development continued: the world's billionaires accumulated five trillion dollars during the pandemic year, while hundreds of millions sank deeper into poverty. These events reveal the dual crisis confronting 21st century democracy – simultaneous threats from authoritarian resurgence and extreme wealth concentration that are not parallel but intertwined (Repucci & Slipowitz, 2021).

By 2025, global billionaire wealth reached $15.8 trillion, exceeding the combined economic output of China and Japan. The richest one percent control 47 percent of global wealth, while the poorest half possesses barely two percent. Meanwhile, Freedom House documents 15 consecutive years of global democratic decline. Extreme wealth concentration actively fuels authoritarian politics through media control, lobbying power, trust erosion, parallel governance structures and digital surveillance infrastructure (UBS, 2025).

Yet this same concentrated wealth funds responses to civilisation's greatest challenges. The Gates Foundation has deployed over 50 billion dollars fighting disease and poverty. MacKenzie Scott has distributed 16 billion dollars to organisations serving marginalised communities. Billionaire-funded initiatives drive breakthroughs in renewable energy, pandemic response and educational innovation. We increasingly rely on unelected philanthropists to address public problems, creating a troubling dependence on private wealth for public purposes (Scott, 2024).

Can extreme wealth serve public purposes without destroying democratic accountability? This book argues we need not accept this false choice. We must reimagine how concentrated wealth relates to democratic governance through the Democratic Wealth Stewardship Framework – reconceptualising extreme wealth not as private property subject only to minimal taxation, but as power requiring robust democratic governance. Wealth holders become temporary stewards of resources with irreducible social origins, not absolute owners with unlimited discretion.

SITUATING THE CONTRIBUTION

This book intervenes in scholarship examining the democratic implications of wealth inequality . Piketty (2014) documented the growth of inequality and proposed wealth taxation, but focused primarily on distributional mechanisms rather than democratic governance frameworks. Reich (2018) powerfully critiqued philanthropic accountability deficits but offered limited systematic alternatives to current foundation governance. Winters (2011) analysed wealth as power and oligarchic wealth defence strategies but emphasised elite preservation of privilege rather than democratic stewardship possibilities. This book develops what prior scholarship identifies but doesn't fully elaborate: a comprehensive democratic governance framework addressing both wealth accumulation (pre-distribution) and philanthropic deployment (post-distribution), while confronting implementation challenges through political-economy analysis. It uniquely integrates authoritarian resilience as a core principle, recognising that concentrated wealth threatens not just equality but democratic survival itself.

THE FRAMEWORK

The framework rests on five principles: reframing property rights as stewardship; ensuring citizens have meaningful roles in overseeing wealth accumulation and deployment; demanding that wealth deployment account for future generations; requiring structures to prevent wealth from enabling authoritarianism; and establishing comprehensive transparency and accountability. These principles work together to create a new relationship between concentrated wealth and democratic authority, while preserving space for innovation and philanthropic initiative.

What wealth threshold triggers democratic stewardship obligations? This framework applies to individuals controlling assets exceeding $50 million and corporations with market capitalisation above $10 billion – levels where wealth becomes systemic power rather than personal security. These thresholds capture roughly the top 0.1% of wealth holders and Fortune 500 companies whose resources shape political outcomes, media landscapes and philanthropic agendas. Stewardship obligations intensify with scale: billionaire wealth faces stricter governance than $100 million fortunes; trillion-dollar corporations face more robust accountability than medium enterprises (Gilens & Page, 2014).

The framework applies to both individual and corporate wealth, though mechanisms differ. It covers wealth across all sectors but imposes sector-specific requirements: technology platforms face enhanced transparency given their information control; natural resource extraction faces intergenerational stewardship obligations given finite resources; the financial sector wealth faces systemic risk oversight given contagion dangers.

This framework is not utopian wishful thinking but responds to emerging political possibilities. Growing populist energy across the political spectrum reflects widespread frustration with elite impunity. Climate urgency creates pressure for massive public investment requiring progressive revenue. Younger generations facing unprecedented wealth barriers show markedly greater openness to structural economic reform. Chapter 11 examines how these dynamics might enable coalition-building among diverse groups – labour, environmentalists, racial justice advocates, small business owners and younger voters – threatened by concentrated wealth's political and economic power.

SCOPE AND STRUCTURE

This book focuses on democratic and democratising states where reforms can be implemented through democratic processes, examining wealth dynamics from 2000 to 2025 with attention to acceleration after 2008 and during COVID-19. It concentrates on three domains: climate change and environmental sustainability, public health and pandemic response and digital technology and information infrastructure.

Part I establishes the crisis. Chapter 1 documents how wealth concentration strengthens authoritarian politics. Chapter 2 presents the innovation-democracy tension. Part II develops the framework. Chapter 3 explicates the five principles with theoretical grounding. Chapter 4 examines historical lessons. Part III analyses wealth's dual nature. Chapter 5 examines philanthropic successes. Chapter 6 identifies democratic deficits. Chapter 7 introduces racial and class dimensions. Part IV presents solutions. Chapter 8 examines pre-distribution mechanisms. Chapter 9 analyses post-distribution governance. Chapter 10 explores participatory innovations. Chapter 11 addresses political economy and implementation.

This is not merely a book about inequality but about power – how concentrated economic power threatens democratic self-governance, and how democracies can govern that power without destroying innovation and philanthropic initiative. If we fail to develop democratic governance of concentrated wealth, we risk losing democracy itself.

Part I

THE CRISIS

1

WEALTH CONCENTRATION AND THE AUTHORITARIAN THREAT

THE SCALE OF CONTEMPORARY WEALTH CONCENTRATION

By 2025, global billionaire wealth reached an unprecedented $15.8 trillion – a figure surpassing the combined gross domestic product of China and Japan, the world's second- and third-largest economies (UBS, 2025). This staggering concentration represents a profound transformation in the distribution of economic resources and, consequently, political power. The wealthiest 1% of humanity now controls 47% of global wealth, while the bottom 50% possesses barely 2% (Credit Suisse, 2024). In the United States, the epicentre of this concentration, the three wealthiest individuals – Elon Musk, Jeff Bezos and Bernard Arnault – collectively hold more wealth than the bottom 50% of American households combined (Institute for Policy Studies, 2024).

Wealth concentration has profoundly racialised dimensions. In the United States, median white family wealth ($188,200) is nearly 8 times median Black family wealth ($24,100) and 5 times median Latino family wealth ($36,100) – gaps rooted in slavery, Jim Crow exclusions from New Deal programmes, redlining and ongoing discrimination (Federal Reserve, 2022). European wealth similarly reflects colonial extraction: Belgian fortunes built on Congolese rubber and minerals, British wealth accumulated through Indian exploitation and French capital derived from Caribbean and African colonies. Contemporary wealth concentration perpetuates these historical injustices through inherited advantage: family wealth finances education, homeownership and business capital that compound across generations. Democratic wealth stewardship must therefore address both current concentration and historical injustices shaping wealth's racial distribution.

This concentration has accelerated dramatically in the 21st century. Between 2000 and 2025, global billionaire wealth increased by 874%, far outpacing global gross domestic product (GDP) growth of 147% over the same period (Bloomberg Billionaires Index, 2025). The COVID-19 pandemic supercharged this trend: while global workers lost $3.7 trillion in earnings during 2020–2021, billionaire wealth surged by $5.5 trillion – a 68% increase in just two years (Oxfam, 2022). The 10 richest men doubled their fortunes from $700 billion to $1.5 trillion during the pandemic, accumulating wealth at a rate of $15,000 per second while 99% of humanity became poorer (Oxfam, 2022).

The sources of this wealth illuminate fundamental changes in the global economy. Technology billionaires dominate the top rankings, with fortunes built on digital platforms, cloud computing, e-commerce and artificial intelligence. Elon Musk's wealth – fluctuating between $180 billion and $250 billion depending on Tesla's stock price – derives primarily from electric vehicles and space technology. Jeff Bezos's $150 billion fortune originates from Amazon's dominance of e-commerce and cloud computing infrastructure. Mark Zuckerberg's $120 billion stems from Meta's control of social media platforms used by over 3 billion people globally (Forbes, 2025).

Beyond technology, wealth concentration extends across sectors. Bernard Arnault's $200 billion luxury goods empire (LVMH) exemplifies concentration in consumer markets. Warren Buffett's $118 billion investment portfolio demonstrates wealth accumulation through financial markets. The Walton family's $220 billion retail fortune (Walmart) shows concentration in traditional commerce (Bloomberg Billionaires Index, 2025).

This extreme wealth concentration is historically unprecedented in democratic societies. While the Gilded Age of the late 19th century saw comparable concentration, that era preceded universal suffrage and modern democratic institutions. Today's concentration occurs within ostensibly democratic systems, creating fundamental tensions between political equality and economic hierarchy. The implications extend far beyond inequality statistics – this concentration transforms democratic governance itself.

INFORMATION CONTROL: BUYING THE PUBLIC SQUARE

The democratic public sphere – the space where citizens deliberate, form opinions and hold power accountable – has been profoundly reshaped by concentrated wealth. Wealthy individuals and corporations now own or control much of the infrastructure through which information flows, from traditional media to digital platforms. This ownership translates into unprecedented power to shape public discourse, set political agendas and influence democratic outcomes.

Traditional media concentration provides the clearest example. In the United States, six corporations – Comcast (NBCUniversal), Disney (ABC), Paramount Global (CBS), Warner Bros. Discovery, Fox Corporation and Sony – control approximately 90% of media consumed by Americans, down from 50 companies in 1983 (Free Press, 2024). Individual billionaires have acquired iconic media institutions: Jeff Bezos purchased The Washington Post in 2013 for $250 million; Rupert Murdoch's News Corp controls The Wall Street Journal, New York Post and Fox News; Marc Benioff acquired Time magazine; and Patrick Soon-Shiong owns the Los Angeles Times.

In India, the Ambani family's Reliance Industries controls major telecom and media properties reaching 400 million subscribers, while the Adani Group's recent media acquisitions raise parallel concerns about billionaire influence over public discourse. South Korea's chaebol – family-controlled conglomerates like Samsung and Hyundai – historically wielded comparable media power, with Samsung's Lee family facing prosecution for using corporate resources to influence political coverage.

These acquisitions grant owners significant influence over editorial direction and political coverage. While most maintain formal editorial independence, ownership shapes content through hiring decisions, resource allocation and strategic priorities. The Washington Post expanded significantly under Bezos's ownership, growing from 580 newsroom staff in 2013 to over 1,000 by 2023, but critics note coverage favourable to Amazon and technology industry interests (Columbia Journalism Review, 2023). Murdoch's media empire has consistently advanced conservative political agendas across multiple countries, wielding outsized influence on electoral outcomes in the United States, the United Kingdom and Australia (Davies, 2014).

Digital platform ownership concentrates informational power even more dramatically. Meta (Facebook, Instagram, WhatsApp) reaches 3.96 billion monthly users – nearly half of humanity – giving Mark Zuckerberg's company unprecedented power to amplify or suppress information (Meta, 2024); Elon Musk's 2022 acquisition of Twitter (rebranded as X) for $44 billion granted him direct control over a platform central to political discourse, journalist communication and real-time news dissemination. Musk's subsequent decisions – reinstating previously banned accounts, altering verification systems and changing content moderation policies – demonstrate how individual billionaire preferences can reshape the information ecosystem overnight (Hern, 2023).

Platform algorithms exercise even deeper informational control. These proprietary systems determine what content billions of users see, shaping attention, emotions and beliefs. Meta's algorithms prioritise content generating 'engagement' (likes, comments, shares), which research shows systematically amplifies divisive, emotional and misleading content over accurate but less sensational information (Shearer, 2021; Vosoughi et al., 2018). YouTube's recommendation algorithm, owned by Google (Alphabet Inc.), influences which videos its 2.7 billion users watch next, creating powerful pathways for radicalisation when algorithms lead viewers towards increasingly extreme content (Ribeiro et al., 2020).

This algorithmic power is exercised without democratic accountability. Platform companies determine content policies unilaterally, deciding what constitutes prohibited hate speech, misinformation or harmful content. These decisions – affecting billions of users across dozens of countries with varied cultural norms and legal frameworks – are made by private companies accountable primarily to shareholders rather than citizens or democratic institutions.

The implications for authoritarian threats are profound. When concentrated wealth controls information infrastructure, authoritarian movements can weaponise these platforms for anti-democratic ends. Facebook's role in facilitating genocide in Myanmar provides a stark example: the platform's algorithms amplified hate speech against Rohingya Muslims, contributing directly to mass atrocities that killed thousands and displaced 700,000 people (United Nations Fact-Finding Mission on Myanmar, 2018). In India, WhatsApp – also owned by Meta – has been used to spread disinformation leading to mob lynchings (Arun, 2019). During the 2016 US presidential election, Facebook's advertising system enabled Russian operatives to target American voters with divisive content, reaching 126 million users with propaganda designed to undermine democratic processes (Mueller, 2019).

Authoritarian governments have learnt to exploit this infrastructure. China's government requires technology companies operating domestically to facilitate surveillance and censorship, turning digital platforms into instruments of state control. Russia has developed sophisticated disinformation capabilities, leveraging Western social media platforms to sow discord in democratic societies. Even in established democracies, the concentration of informational power in private hands creates vulnerabilities that authoritarian movements exploit.

The 6 January 2021 insurrection at the US Capitol illustrates these dynamics. Social media platforms – particularly Facebook, Twitter and YouTube – served as primary organising infrastructure for groups coordinating the attack.

Misinformation about the 2020 election spread rapidly through platform algorithms optimised for engagement rather than accuracy. Parler, a platform marketed to conservatives, became a key coordination hub when mainstream platforms began moderating election misinformation, demonstrating how fragmented platform governance creates accountability gaps (Aliapoulios et al., 2021).

Information control through concentrated wealth undermines democracy's epistemic foundations – the shared factual basis necessary for democratic deliberation. When billionaires control information infrastructure, democratic discourse occurs on terrain shaped by private interests rather than public purposes.

Policy Capture: When Money Speaks Louder Than Votes

Extreme wealth concentration translates into policy influence through multiple mechanisms: campaign finance, lobbying, revolving doors between government and industry, and think tank funding. This influence systematically skews policy outcomes towards the preferences of economic elites, creating what political scientists Martin Gilens and Benjamin Page (2014) term 'economic elite domination' rather than democratic representation.

CAMPAIGN FINANCE AS POLITICAL INVESTMENT

In the United States, the Supreme Court's Citizens United v. FEC (2010) decision eliminated restrictions on independent political expenditures by corporations and wealthy individuals, unleashing a flood of money into electoral politics. Super political action committees (PACs) can now raise unlimited funds from wealthy donors, corporations and unions to support or oppose candidates. The results are stark: in the 2020 election cycle, the top 100 donors contributed $1.9 billion – more than the combined contributions of 4.6 million small donors giving less than $200 each (OpenSecrets, 2021). The 2024 election cycle saw even greater concentration, with the top 50 donors contributing over $2.5 billion (OpenSecrets, 2025).

Individual mega-donors exercise outsized influence. In 2022, billionaire Sam Bankman-Fried contributed over $40 million to Democratic candidates and causes, making him the party's second-largest donor before his cryptocurrency empire collapsed amid fraud charges. Peter Thiel contributed over $35 million supporting Republican Senate candidates, directly shaping GOP primary outcomes (Vogel, 2022). The Walton family (Walmart) and Koch network consistently rank among the top political contributors, directing hundreds of millions towards candidates and causes aligned with their business interests.

This money purchases access and influence. Major donors receive private meetings with candidates, shape party platforms, influence cabinet appointments and gain direct channels to policymakers. While quid pro quo corruption (explicit vote-buying) is illegal, the subtler dynamics of access, relationship-building and ideological alignment systematically advantage wealthy donors' policy preferences.

The effects extend beyond elections. Wealthy donors fund ballot initiative campaigns, enabling them to bypass legislatures and directly shape state policy. In California, the 2020 Proposition 22 – exempting gig economy companies from classifying workers as employees – was backed by $200 million from Uber, Lyft, DoorDash, Instacart and Postmates, making it the most expensive ballot measure in US history (Scheiber & Conger, 2020). The companies prevailed, securing policy outcomes protecting their business models despite legislative attempts at worker protection.

LOBBYING AS POLICY INFLUENCE

Beyond campaign contributions, corporate lobbying dwarfs other forms of policy advocacy. In 2023, corporations and industry associations spent $4.2 billion on lobbying – 15 times the $280 million spent by labour unions, public interest groups and all other non-corporate interests combined (OpenSecrets, 2024). This disparity reflects fundamental imbalances in organised political representation.

The US Chamber of Commerce alone spent $81 million on lobbying in 2023, making it the single largest spender. Pharmaceutical Research and Manufacturers of America (PhRMA) spent $27 million, the American Hospital Association $24 million and the Business Roundtable $22 million. Individual corporations also maintain massive lobbying operations: Amazon spent $21 million, Meta (Facebook) $20 million and Alphabet (Google) $13 million on direct lobbying in 2023 (OpenSecrets, 2024).

European wealth exercises policy influence through different mechanisms. Germany's Mittelstand families and France's grandes fortunes maintain dense networks within elite educational institutions (ENA, Sciences Po) that supply political leadership. In Brazil, construction conglomerates shaped infrastructure policy through systematic corruption exposed in the Lava Jato investigations. Japan's keiretsu system embeds corporate influence within bureaucratic policymaking through amakudari (descent from heaven), whereby retired officials join companies they once regulated.

This spending purchases sophisticated policy influence. Corporate lobbyists often write legislative language that friendly lawmakers introduce as bills. They provide 'technical expertise' shaping regulatory implementation. They fund research supporting industry-favourable policy conclusions. They finance front groups and astroturf campaigns, creating the appearance of grassroots support for corporate-friendly policies. They deploy armies of former government officials – leveraging relationships and insider knowledge – to advance client interests.

The revolving door between government and industry compounds this influence. Former members of Congress, congressional staff and executive branch officials routinely become lobbyists, trading on connections and expertise developed in public service. Between 2009 and 2020, 65% of senators and 43% of representatives who left Congress became lobbyists (OpenSecrets, 2021). This pathway incentivises policymakers to cultivate industry relationships while in office, anticipating lucrative private sector employment.

POLICY OUTCOMES: ELITE PREFERENCES TRUMP PUBLIC OPINION

The cumulative effect of campaign finance and lobbying is a systematic policy skew favouring economic elites. Gilens and Page's (2014) landmark study analysed 1,779 policy issues, comparing policy outcomes to the preferences of average citizens, economic elites and organised interest groups. Their stark finding: 'economic elites and organised groups representing business interests have substantial independent impacts on U.S. government policy, while average citizens and mass-based interest groups have little or no independent influence' (Gilens & Page, 2014, p. 565).

When economic elites support a policy, it has about a 45% chance of being adopted, regardless of what average citizens want. When economic elites oppose a policy, it has less than an 18% chance of adoption, regardless of public support. Average citizens' preferences only matter when they align with elite preferences; when they diverge, elite preferences prevail (Gilens & Page, 2014).

This pattern appears across policy domains. Tax policy consistently favours high earners: the 2017 Tax Cuts and Jobs Act delivered 83% of its benefits to the top 1% of earners by 2027, despite public polling showing majority opposition to tax cuts for the wealthy (Institute on Taxation and Economic Policy, 2018; Pew Research Center, 2017). Financial regulation systematically weakened after industry lobbying: the Dodd-Frank Wall Street Reform Act of 2010 was substantially diluted through subsequent legislation in 2018, despite public support for strong financial regulation following the 2008 crisis. Labour law reform perennially stalls despite majority public support for collective bargaining rights, reflecting corporate opposition to unionisation (Pew Research Center, 2022).

Healthcare policy illustrates these dynamics particularly clearly. Pharmaceutical companies spent over $370 million lobbying between 2019 and 2021, successfully blocking proposals to allow Medicare to negotiate drug prices – a policy supported by 83% of Americans across partisan lines (West Health-Gallup, 2021). When Congress finally passed limited negotiation authority in the 2022 Inflation Reduction Act, it applied to only 10 drugs initially, far weaker than public preferences or original proposals (Congressional Budget Office, 2022).

Climate policy shows similar patterns. Fossil fuel companies spent over $2 billion on lobbying and campaign contributions between 2000 and 2020, systematically weakening or blocking climate legislation despite growing public concern about climate change (InfluenceMap, 2021). When Congress passed the 2022 Inflation Reduction Act – the most significant US climate legislation to date – fossil fuel interests secured major concessions, including requirements for new oil and gas lease sales as a condition for renewable energy development (Friedman & Tankersley, 2022).

Policy capture extends internationally. Multinational corporations leverage their footprint across jurisdictions to play countries against each other, threatening to relocate operations unless governments provide favourable tax treatment, environmental exemptions or labour law carve-outs. This dynamic creates race-to-the-bottom pressures, systematically undermining democratic policy preferences regarding taxation, environmental protection and worker rights.

TRUST EROSION: THE LEGITIMACY CRISIS

The visible influence of concentrated wealth on democratic processes erodes public trust in democratic institutions, creating openings for authoritarian populists who promise to 'drain the swamp' and restore government accountability. This erosion represents a fundamental threat to democratic stability: democracy requires citizens to believe that political institutions respond to their interests and that elections offer meaningful choices. When citizens perceive government as captured by economic elites, they become vulnerable to anti-democratic alternatives promising disruption.

Public trust in government has collapsed across established democracies. In the United States, trust in the federal government fell from 73% in 1958 to just 16% by 2023 – near historic lows (Pew Research Center, 2023). Similar patterns appear across Organisation for Economic Co-operation and Development (OECD) countries: average trust in national governments declined from 45% in 2007 to 41% by 2021, with particularly steep drops following the 2008 financial crisis and COVID-19 pandemic (OECD, 2022). In France, trust in the National Assembly fell to 29% by 2024; in the United Kingdom, trust in Parliament dropped to 28%; in Spain, trust in the Cortes reached just 24% (Edelman Trust Barometer, 2024).

This erosion correlates strongly with perceptions of elite capture. Cross-national surveys consistently show that citizens who believe 'government is run by big interests looking out for themselves' express dramatically lower trust in democratic institutions than those who believe 'government is run for the benefit of all people' (Pew Research Center, 2021). In the United States, 71% of Republicans and 66% of Democrats agreed in 2023 that 'government is run by a small number of big interests', up from 53% and 54%, respectively, in 1994 (Pew Research Center, 2023).

Trust erosion follows racialised patterns. Black and Latino Americans express systematically lower trust in government institutions than white Americans, reflecting lived experiences of discriminatory policing, unequal service provision and policy neglect (Pew Research Center, 2021). When communities of colour observe white elites capturing policy outcomes while their neighbourhoods lack basic services, perceived system illegitimacy deepens, creating distinct vulnerabilities to both left and right populist appeals.

Media reporting on policy capture reinforces these perceptions. High-profile examples – wealthy individuals receiving enormous tax breaks, financial institutions escaping meaningful accountability after causing the 2008 crisis, pharmaceutical companies blocking drug price negotiation – create vivid narratives of system failure. The International Consortium of Investigative Journalists, 2016 (Panama Papers) and International Consortium of Investigative Journalists, 2021 (Pandora Papers) revealed how wealthy elites systematically evade taxation through offshore havens, generating widespread outrage about unequal treatment under the law.

Economic inequality itself feeds trust erosion. Research by political scientists Yotam Margalit and Luis Vega (2023) demonstrates that rising inequality reduces political trust independently of other factors. As citizens observe growing gaps between their economic circumstances and those of elites, they increasingly doubt whether democratic institutions serve broad public interests. This perception is self-reinforcing: low trust reduces civic participation, further enabling elite influence, which generates more visible capture, deepening distrust.

The legitimacy crisis creates fertile ground for authoritarian populism. Authoritarian leaders exploit distrust by positioning themselves as outsiders who will dismantle corrupt elite systems. Donald Trump's 2016 campaign explicitly leveraged this dynamic, promising to 'drain the swamp' of Washington corruption and attacking 'crooked Hillary Clinton' as embodying elite impunity. Brazil's Jair Bolsonaro, Hungary's Viktor Orbán, the Philippines' Rodrigo Duterte and India's Narendra Modi all employed similar anti-elite rhetoric, channelling legitimate grievances about captured governance towards authoritarian solutions that ultimately concentrate rather than disperse power.

Ironically, many authoritarian populists are themselves economic elites or closely allied with concentrated wealth. Trump entered office with an estimated net worth of $2.5 billion and appointed multiple billionaires to cabinet positions (Forbes, 2017). Italy's Silvio Berlusconi was a billionaire media mogul. Yet their anti-elite rhetoric resonated with voters disillusioned by visible policy capture, demonstrating how trust erosion creates vulnerabilities that demagogues exploit.

Once in power, authoritarian populists frequently deepen rather than address the underlying dynamics. They attack independent institutions (judiciary, media, civil service) that might constrain executive power or hold elites accountable. They reward loyal oligarchs while punishing opponents, personalising rather than democratising governance. They use their mandates to consolidate power rather than disperse it, replacing one form of elite control with another – often more arbitrary and less constrained by law.

Research by political scientists Roberto Stefan Foa and Yascha Mounk (2016, 2017) documents how declining confidence in democracy correlates with authoritarian stability. In the United States, citizens expressing satisfaction with democracy fell from 79% in 1995 to 50% by 2023, with particularly sharp declines among younger cohorts (World Values Survey, 2023). Across European democracies, citizens willing to consider authoritarian alternatives rose from 23% in 1995 to 32% by 2020 (Foa et al., 2020).

While most citizens remain committed to democratic norms, erosion at the margins creates openings for anti-democratic movements.

PARALLEL GOVERNANCE: THE PRIVATISATION OF PUBLIC PURPOSE

Large foundations and philanthropic organisations increasingly function as parallel governance structures, making decisions about public priorities without democratic authorisation or accountability. This 'privatization of public purpose' (Reich, 2018) represents a fundamental challenge to democratic sovereignty: when private wealth determines which problems receive attention, which solutions are attempted and how public goods are delivered, democratic citizens lose control over collective priorities.

The scale of modern philanthropy is unprecedented. US foundations held \$1.4 trillion in assets by 2024, with annual giving exceeding \$105 billion (Foundation Center, 2025). The Bill & Melinda Gates Foundation alone controls over \$70 billion in assets – larger than the gross domestic product (GDP) of 120 countries – and distributes approximately \$6 billion annually (Bill & Melinda Gates Foundation, 2024). Other mega-foundations include the Ford Foundation (\$16 billion in assets), the William and Flora Hewlett Foundation (\$13 billion), the Wellcome Trust (\$37 billion) and the Open Society Foundations (\$25 billion) (Foundation Directory Online, 2024).

These foundations exercise substantial power over global policy domains. The Gates Foundation dominates global health governance, providing approximately 12% of the World Health Organization's budget by 2023 – making it the second-largest donor after Germany and ahead of most countries (World Health Organization (WHO), 2023). This funding gives Gates substantial influence over WHO priorities, research agendas and intervention strategies, despite zero democratic accountability to the billions of people affected by these decisions.

In education, the Gates Foundation has fundamentally shaped US public education policy. Between 2000 and 2020, the foundation spent over \$5 billion on K-12 education initiatives in the United States, funding everything from charter school expansion to Common Core State Standards implementation to teacher evaluation systems (Barkan, 2018; Reckhow, 2013). Many of these initiatives proved controversial or unsuccessful, yet they were implemented across thousands of schools, affecting millions of students based primarily on Gates's personal education theories rather than democratic deliberation.

The Chan Zuckerberg Initiative (CZI) – established by Mark Zuckerberg and Priscilla Chan with $45 billion in Facebook stock – exemplifies contemporary mega-philanthropy's parallel governance. Structured as a limited liability company (LLC) rather than a traditional foundation, CZI faces minimal regulatory oversight while pursuing goals spanning education, criminal justice reform, affordable housing and disease eradication. Its scale and scope match many government agencies, but it operates according to founders' priorities rather than democratic mandates.

The structural problem is accountability. Foundations are legally accountable only to boards they control, not to the communities they affect. Unlike democratic governments answerable to voters, foundations answer only to donors and trustees – typically drawn from elite networks sharing similar worldviews. Foundation staff, no matter how well-intentioned, are not elected representatives but appointed professionals implementing donor visions.

This creates what political theorist Rob Reich (2018) calls a 'governance gap': foundations exercise power over public priorities without democratic legitimation. They decide which diseases receive research funding, which educational approaches are promoted, which communities receive investment, and which social problems warrant attention – all without consulting those affected. When foundation initiatives fail, as many do, there is no electoral accountability, no democratic correction mechanism and often no systematic learning or course correction.

The participatory deficit is equally troubling. Foundation grantmaking typically operates through competitive processes where organisations propose projects aligned with foundation priorities. This structures relationships hierarchically: foundations set agendas, and non-profits conform to access funding. Community voices are filtered through non-profit professionals rather than expressed directly. Participatory grantmaking models – where community members directly allocate resources – remain rare, accounting for less than 2% of foundation giving (Participatory Grantmaking Community, 2023).

Democratic foundation oversight might include: mandatory participatory grantmaking for at least 25% of distributions, with community members directly allocating resources; community representation comprising at least one-third of foundation boards, selected through democratic processes rather than trustee appointment; democratic review panels assessing mega-foundation strategic priorities every five years, with authority to recommend modifications; sunset provisions requiring foundations exceeding $10 billion in assets to obtain periodic democratic reauthorisation; comprehensive transparency requirements including full disclosure of grantmaking rationale, denied applications and evaluation findings. Chapter 9 develops these mechanisms in detail.

Donor-advised funds (DAFs) compound these accountability problems. DAFs allow donors to take immediate tax deductions while retaining indefinite control over when and how funds are distributed. By 2024, DAFs held over $250 billion – exceeding total assets of the largest private foundations combined – yet face minimal distribution requirements and virtually no transparency obligations (National Philanthropic Trust, 2024). Donors can effectively warehouse wealth tax-free in perpetuity while maintaining control over eventual deployment, creating permanent parallel governance structures without even the minimal accountability requirements facing private foundations.

International development philanthropy raises particularly acute sovereignty concerns. When the Gates Foundation spends billions on African agriculture through its Alliance for a Green Revolution in Africa (AGRA), it shapes food systems, land use policies and seed markets across the continent. Critics charge that AGRA's emphasis on commercial seeds and chemical fertilisers advances a Western industrial agriculture model misaligned with African farmers' interests and ecological sustainability. Yet these decisions – affecting hundreds of millions of people – are made in Seattle by foundation staff, not by African communities or democratic institutions.

Climate philanthropy follows similar patterns. While mega-foundations like Bloomberg Philanthropies, the Hewlett Foundation and the ClimateWorks Foundation have channelled billions towards climate action, they determine priorities: renewable energy versus adaptation, market mechanisms versus regulatory approaches and technological solutions versus consumption reduction. These are inherently political choices with winners and losers, yet they occur in foundations' private decision-making rather than democratic deliberation.

The dependency trap further erodes democratic governance. When public services become dependent on philanthropic funding, governments cede priority-setting to donors. Public schools reliant on foundation grants must align programmes with donor preferences. Public health systems dependent on Gates funding must accommodate foundation priorities. This shifts accountability: officials are responsive to foundation programme officers rather than democratic constituencies.

Parallel governance ultimately hollows out democratic capacity. When private wealth substitutes for public investment, it reduces pressure for adequate taxation and public service provision. It normalises the idea that public goods depend on elite generosity rather than democratic entitlement. It creates a two-tier system: basic services for most and enhanced foundation-funded services for selected communities. This corrodes democratic solidarity and entrenches elite power over collective futures.

Yet wealth concentration also creates its own opposition. As the following chapters demonstrate, successful wealth governance reforms – from New Deal taxation to post-war social democracy – emerged from political coalitions built during prior crisis periods. Today's converging crises may similarly create openings for democratic wealth stewardship that seem impossible under normal politics.

2

THE INNOVATION-DEMOCRACY TENSION

CRISIS CONVERGENCE IN THE 2020s

The 2020s have witnessed an unprecedented convergence of global crises demanding urgent, coordinated responses: accelerating climate change, collapsing biodiversity, disruptive artificial intelligence (AI), widening social inequality and democratic backsliding. Each crisis alone would test governance capacity; together, they create compounding pressures that expose fundamental tensions between the pace of change and the speed of democratic deliberation.

CLIMATE EMERGENCY

By 2025, global temperatures had risen 1.3°C above pre-industrial levels, approaching the 1.5°C threshold that scientists identify as a critical tipping point (Intergovernmental Panel on Climate Change [IPCC], 2023). The consequences are increasingly visible: record-breaking heatwaves killed thousands across Europe, South Asia and North America; catastrophic floods displaced millions in Pakistan, Nigeria and China; unprecedented wildfires consumed vast territories in Australia, Canada, Greece and California; and prolonged droughts threatened food security across East Africa and the Mediterranean (World Meteorological Organization, 2024).

The window for preventing catastrophic warming is rapidly closing. The IPCC's Sixth Assessment Report (2023) concluded that limiting warming to 1.5°C requires global emissions to peak by 2025 and decline by 43% by

2030 – a pace of transformation unprecedented in economic history. Achieving net-zero emissions by 2050 requires restructuring energy systems, transportation networks, agricultural practices and industrial processes globally within just three decades.

Yet democratic responses have lagged alarmingly behind scientific imperatives. The United Nations Framework Convention on Climate Change (UNFCCC) process, operating since 1992, has produced incremental agreements that failed to bend the emissions curve. The 2015 Paris Agreement represented progress, but voluntary national commitments remained insufficient: current policies put the world on track for approximately 2.7°C warming by 2100 – far beyond safe limits (Climate Action Tracker, 2024). Legislative action in major emitting countries has been delayed by partisan gridlock, industry lobbying and electoral cycles prioritising short-term concerns over long-term survival.

These dynamics play out differently across welfare state regimes. Social democratic systems (Scandinavia, the Netherlands) maintained stronger wealth taxation and public service provision, moderating – though not eliminating – concentration trends. Conservative welfare states (Germany, France, Japan) preserved middle-class stability through employment protection but permitted wealth accumulation at the top. Liberal regimes (US, United Kingdom (UK)) experienced the sharpest concentration as financialisation and deregulation accelerated. Southern European democracies faced austerity-driven inequality increases during the Eurozone crisis. These regime differences suggest that wealth stewardship implementation will require context-specific adaptations rather than universal prescriptions.

BIODIVERSITY COLLAPSE

The Living Planet Index shows a 69% average decline in monitored wildlife populations since 1970, driven by habitat destruction, pollution, overexploitation, climate change and invasive species (WWF, 2022). Scientists warn of a sixth mass extinction event – the first caused by human activity – with species disappearing at 100–1,000 times the natural background rate (Intergovernmental Science-Policy Platform on Biodiversity and Ecosystem Services (IPBES), 2019). By 2025, over 42,000 species faced extinction risk according to the International Union for Conservation of Nature (IUCN) Red List, including 41% of amphibians, 36% of reef-building corals, 27% of mammals and 13% of birds (IUCN, 2024).

Ecosystem services worth an estimated $125–$140 trillion annually – pollination, water purification, climate regulation, soil formation – are degrading rapidly (Costanza et al., 2014; Dasgupta, 2021). Ocean acidification threatens marine food chains supporting billions of people. Insect populations, foundational to terrestrial ecosystems, have declined by 75% in some monitored regions over the past 50 years (Hallmann et al., 2017). Tropical forests, housing 80% of terrestrial biodiversity, continue shrinking at rates exceeding 10 million hectares annually (Food and Agriculture Organization (FAO), 2020).

Democratic governance has proven inadequate to this challenge. International conventions on biodiversity (Convention on Biological Diversity (CBD), Convention on International Trade in Endangered Species (CITES)) lack enforcement mechanisms. National policies frequently prioritise economic development over ecosystem protection. The 2022 Kunming-Montreal Global Biodiversity Framework set ambitious targets – protecting 30% of land and sea by 2030 – but implementation remains uncertain, underfunded and vulnerable to political reversal (Convention on Biological Diversity [CBD], 2022).

ARTIFICIAL INTELLIGENCE DISRUPTION

AI capabilities have advanced with breathtaking speed. Large language models like GPT-4 (released 2023) demonstrate reasoning, creativity and problem-solving approaching human levels in many domains. AI systems now exceed human performance in image recognition, strategic game-playing, protein folding prediction and specialised medical diagnostics. By 2025, AI applications had permeated industries from healthcare and finance to transportation and manufacturing, promising productivity gains but threatening widespread job displacement (DeepMind, 2024; OpenAI, 2023).

The pace of AI development vastly exceeds regulatory capacity. GPT-4 was released without comprehensive safety testing or impact assessment. Autonomous weapon systems are being deployed by militaries worldwide without international agreements governing their use. Facial recognition and predictive policing algorithms are implemented by law enforcement agencies despite documented racial bias and surveillance concerns. Social media recommendation algorithms, powered by increasingly sophisticated AI, shape billions of people's information environments without democratic oversight (Crawford, 2021).

The governance gap is particularly acute because AI development is concentrated in a handful of private corporations – primarily Google (DeepMind, Google AI), Microsoft (OpenAI partnership), Meta (FAIR), Amazon (AWS AI) and Anthropic – whose priorities reflect shareholder value maximisation rather than public interest. These companies make fundamental choices about AI safety, bias mitigation, transparency and deployment with minimal democratic input. When OpenAI's board briefly removed CEO Sam Altman in November 2023 over safety concerns, the decision was reversed within days following pressure from investors and employees – illustrating that corporate governance, not democratic deliberation, determines AI trajectory (Knight, 2023).

Authoritarian regimes have aggressively deployed AI for social control. China's social credit system uses AI-powered surveillance to monitor and score citizens' behaviour, restricting travel, employment and educational opportunities based on political compliance (Creemers, 2018). Facial recognition systems track Uyghurs in Xinjiang as part of a campaign the UN described as potentially constituting crimes against humanity (Office of the United Nations High Commissioner for Human Rights [OHCHR], 2022). Russia and other authoritarian states use AI to identify dissidents, predict protests and target opposition movements. Democratic societies face an AI arms race: failing to develop advanced AI risks military and economic disadvantage, yet developing it without adequate safeguards creates domestic surveillance threats and global instability.

SOCIAL INEQUALITY

As documented in Chapter 1, wealth concentration reached historic extremes by 2025. But beyond raw wealth gaps, multidimensional inequality – in health, education, political influence, intergenerational mobility and life expectancy – has widened across and within countries. In the United States, life expectancy at birth differs by over 20 years between the richest and poorest counties (Dwyer-Lindgren et al., 2017). Educational opportunity increasingly depends on parental wealth: children from top-income quintile families are seven times more likely to complete college than children from bottom-quintile families (Chetty et al., 2017).

Geographic inequality compounds these disparities. In many countries, prosperity concentrates in capital cities and technology hubs, while peripheral regions experience population decline, service cutbacks and economic stagnation. In the United States, five metropolitan areas – San Francisco, Seattle, San Jose, Boston and San Diego – captured 90% of technology sector job growth between 2005 and 2017, while most of the country experienced minimal tech employment gains (Muro et al., 2019). Similar patterns appear across Europe, where Paris, London, Berlin and Stockholm pull away from shrinking industrial cities and rural areas.

Rising inequality fuels political polarisation and anti-democratic movements. Research demonstrates that economic insecurity and relative deprivation correlate strongly with support for authoritarian populists across democracies (Gest et al., 2018; Norris & Inglehart, 2019). The perception that democratic institutions serve elite interests while ignoring working-class concerns creates fertile ground for demagogues promising disruption.

DEMOCRATIC EROSION

Freedom House's annual Freedom in the World report documented democratic decline for 17 consecutive years through 2023, with more countries experiencing deterioration than improvement each year since 2006 (Freedom House, 2024). The number of countries classified as 'Free' fell from 89 in 2006 to 79 by 2023, while 'Not Free' countries increased from 42 to 52 over the same period. Even established democracies experienced backsliding: the United States, India, Brazil, Hungary, Poland and Turkey all saw declining freedom scores between 2015 and 2023.

Authoritarian tactics have become more sophisticated. Rather than staging overt coups, contemporary autocrats hollow out democratic institutions from within through legal means: packing courts, attacking independent media, restricting civil society, manipulating electoral rules and deploying targeted disinformation (Levitsky & Ziblatt, 2018; Runciman, 2018). This 'authoritarian legalism' maintains democratic façades while concentrating power (Scheppele, 2018).

The proliferation of hybrid regimes – neither fully democratic nor overtly authoritarian – represents a particularly concerning trend. Countries like Russia, Turkey, Hungary, Venezuela and Nicaragua maintain electoral institutions but systematically manipulate them to prevent genuine opposition victories. These regimes demonstrate that elections alone do not guarantee democracy; meaningful contestation, accountability and rights protections are equally essential.

THE INNOVATION-DEMOCRACY TENSION

This crisis convergence exposes a fundamental tension: the mechanisms of democratic deliberation – debate, coalition-building, compromise, electoral cycles – operate slowly compared to the pace of technological change, environmental deterioration and authoritarian adaptation. This temporal mismatch creates pressure to bypass democratic processes in favour of faster technocratic or authoritarian approaches.

DEFENDING INNOVATION THROUGH DEMOCRATIC WEALTH STEWARDSHIP

Defenders argue that concentrated wealth enables innovation: SpaceX achieved reusable rockets while NASA faced bureaucratic constraints; the Gates Foundation deployed malaria interventions governments neglected; and venture capital funded transformative startups governments couldn't. These claims merit examination.

First, public investment historically drove breakthrough innovation: the Internet emerged from DARPA, GPS from military research, touchscreens from government grants and mRNA vaccines from NIH funding and German public research. Private wealth commercialised publicly funded discoveries.

Second, innovation requires adequate resources, not concentrated wealth specifically. Postwar America achieved extraordinary innovation (1945–1975) despite top marginal tax rates of 70–91% and relatively compressed wealth distribution. Sweden, with robust wealth taxation, leads global innovation indices.

Third, concentrated wealth may impede innovation by monopolising talent, acquiring potential competitors and directing resources towards profitable applications rather than socially optimal ones. Democratic wealth stewardship can preserve innovation incentives through adequate rewards for successful entrepreneurship while preventing concentration that distorts democratic processes. The question is not wealth versus innovation but rather what wealth distribution best balances innovation with democratic accountability.

THE SPEED DIFFERENTIAL

Technology companies operate on innovation cycles measured in months or weeks. OpenAI developed GPT-4 in approximately 18 months. Google's DeepMind solved the 50-year protein folding problem in 2020 and then dramatically improved its AlphaFold system within two years. Tesla regularly updates vehicle software remotely, adding new autonomous driving capabilities to millions of cars virtually overnight. Social media platforms implement algorithmic changes affecting billions of users without notice or consultation.

By contrast, democratic legislative processes operate on timescales of years or decades. The European Union's General Data Protection Regulation (GDPR) – widely considered the world's most comprehensive digital privacy framework – took six years from initial proposal (2012) to implementation (2018). The US Congress has not passed major privacy legislation despite decades of advocacy. AI regulation remains minimal globally: as of 2025, only the European Union (EU)'s AI Act (finalised in 2024 after 3 years of negotiation) provided comprehensive AI governance, with implementation extending through 2027 (European Parliament, 2024).

This temporal mismatch creates regulatory lag. By the time democratic institutions establish rules, technology has evolved beyond the original framework. Social media regulation developed in response to Facebook's 2016 election interference proved inadequate for newer platforms like TikTok. Privacy regulations designed for web browsing struggle to address AI-powered behavioural prediction. Autonomous vehicle safety standards drafted for highway driving fail to anticipate complex urban deployment scenarios.

Climate governance faces similar temporal challenges. Democratic electoral cycles spanning 2–6 years create incentives for politicians to prioritise immediate concerns over long-term climate action whose benefits accrue decades hence. Climate policies often require upfront costs (carbon taxes, fossil fuel restrictions, infrastructure investment), while benefits (avoided warming, prevented disasters) are diffuse and temporally distant. This temporal mismatch systematically disadvantages climate action in democratic competition against opponents offering immediate economic relief or cultural grievance politics.

THE SCALE CHALLENGE

Many contemporary crises are inherently global, yet democratic governance remains predominantly national. Climate change, biodiversity loss, pandemic disease, AI safety, financial instability and tax evasion all transcend national borders, yet an effective response requires coordinated action across dozens or hundreds of countries with divergent interests, political systems and development levels.

International cooperation mechanisms – the United Nations, World Trade Organization, International Monetary Fund, World Health Organization – operate primarily through consensus or weak enforcement, rendering them vulnerable to veto by individual states or blocs. The UN Security Council's permanent member veto system paralyses action on conflicts where great powers have interests. The WTO's dispute resolution system has been crippled since 2019 when the US blocked appellate body appointments. The WHO lacks authority to compel pandemic response coordination, as COVID-19 demonstrated when countries pursued uncoordinated national strategies.

Private actors increasingly fill this governance vacuum. Technology companies establish de facto global standards through platform design: Facebook's content moderation policies functionally regulate speech for 3 billion users across 190 countries. Google's search algorithm determines information accessibility globally. Apple's and Google's smartphone operating systems set privacy defaults affecting billions of devices worldwide. These companies make what are effectively global governance decisions unilaterally, based on corporate priorities rather than democratic deliberation.

In climate action, private sector initiatives often move faster than democratic governments. Corporate renewable energy commitments exceeded government mandates in many jurisdictions by 2024. Major corporations – Apple, Google, Microsoft, Amazon – achieved operational carbon neutrality years before national net-zero targets. Investment firms like BlackRock and financial institutions like JPMorgan Chase incorporated climate risk into capital allocation decisions, shifting trillions in investment ahead of regulatory requirements (Fink, 2022; Task Force on Climate-related Financial Disclosures, 2023).

Philanthropic organisations similarly operate at a global scale with minimal democratic oversight. The Gates Foundation's global health programs span over 100 countries. The Open Society Foundations promote democracy and human rights across six continents. The Wellcome Trust funds biomedical research globally. These organisations make resource allocation decisions affecting millions or billions of people based on trustee priorities rather than democratic mandates from affected populations.

THE EXPERTISE PROBLEM

Contemporary challenges increasingly involve technical complexity requiring specialised expertise: climate science, epidemiology, AI safety, genomic medicine and financial engineering. Democratic citizens cannot be expected to master these domains sufficiently to make informed policy judgements through direct participation. This creates pressure for technocratic governance – rule by experts – that potentially sidelines democratic deliberation.

The tension between expertise and democracy is not new, but contemporary crises intensify it. Climate policy requires integrating atmospheric physics, oceanography, ecology, economics, engineering and social science – knowledge distributed across multiple expert communities with different methodologies, assumptions and normative commitments. AI safety research involves computer science, cognitive science, philosophy and political theory. Pandemic response demands expertise in epidemiology, virology, public health, logistics and behavioural science.

Experts themselves often disagree, reflecting genuine scientific uncertainty, different disciplinary perspectives and varying normative assumptions embedded in technical analysis. During COVID-19, epidemiologists debated infection fatality rates, the effectiveness of various interventions and optimal policy responses. Climate scientists debate carbon budget calculations and the feasibility of specific mitigation pathways. AI researchers disagree fundamentally about whether advanced AI poses existential risks or constitutes overblown speculation.

These disagreements create opportunities for motivated reasoning and strategic expertise deployment. Actors seeking to delay climate action cite minority scientific opinions questioning consensus findings. Opponents of pandemic restrictions emphasise studies showing intervention costs while downplaying benefit estimates. Technology companies fund research concluding that algorithmic regulation would stifle innovation. Separating genuine expertise from interested advocacy becomes increasingly difficult for democratic publics.

Yet democratic accountability demands that citizens, not just experts, shape fundamental value choices embedded in technical decisions. Climate policy involves inherent trade-offs: present versus future welfare, economic growth versus ecological protection, national versus global priorities and technological optimism versus precautionary principles. These are political choices that technical expertise alone cannot resolve. AI governance requires balancing innovation benefits against risks of job displacement, surveillance and loss of human agency – again, political choices not reducible to technical optimisation.

The challenge is integrating expertise with democratic legitimacy: enabling citizens to exercise meaningful control over policy direction while incorporating specialised knowledge essential for effective implementation. Democratic wealth stewardship must navigate this tension, ensuring that concentrated private wealth does not use technical complexity as a shield against democratic accountability while recognising that effective governance requires sophisticated technical capacity.

THE AUTHORITARIAN ALTERNATIVE

Some observers argue that authoritarian systems handle these challenges more effectively than democracies. China's government mandated rapid deployment of renewable energy, electric vehicles and high-speed rail without the delays inherent in democratic deliberation. During COVID-19, China implemented strict lockdowns that many democracies struggled to sustain politically. China's social credit system and comprehensive surveillance infrastructure enabled rapid contact tracing that Western democracies could not replicate due to privacy protections and civil liberties constraints.

These observations contain partial truth but miss essential dynamics. First, authoritarian effectiveness is selective and often overstated. China's initial COVID-19 response involved censoring doctors who warned about the outbreak, delaying global notification and suppressing information – failures that enabled the virus' global spread. China's debt-fuelled infrastructure investments generated waste, corruption and financial instability. Environmental regulations are systematically unenforced when they conflict with local economic interests. The efficiency narrative often reflects authoritarian control of information more than actual policy effectiveness.

Second, authoritarian systems lack self-correction mechanisms. Democracies course-correct through electoral accountability, media scrutiny, civil society advocacy and institutional checks. When democratic policies fail, opposition forces mobilise, the media investigate and elections provide correction opportunities. Authoritarian systems suppress feedback mechanisms, enabling errors to compound unchecked. China's zero-COVID policy continued long past the point where costs clearly exceeded benefits because no institutional mechanism allowed course correction until Xi Jinping personally changed direction in late 2022.

Third, authoritarian governance involves systematic rights violations that democracies properly reject. China's Xinjiang surveillance system – cited as a model of technological governance – enables cultural genocide against Uyghurs. Social credit systems punish political dissent alongside fraud and traffic violations, collapsing criminal justice and political control. These are not unfortunate side effects but core features: authoritarian 'efficiency' depends on crushing dissent and individual autonomy.

Fourth, authoritarian states increasingly weaponise their technological and economic power to undermine democracies globally. China exports surveillance technology to authoritarian regimes worldwide. Russia deploys social media manipulation and cyberattacks against democratic processes. The authoritarian alternative is not merely a different governance model but an active threat to democratic survival.

The innovation-democracy tension is real, but the authoritarian solution trades democratic values for illusory efficiency while creating new authoritarian threats. Democratic wealth stewardship offers a different path: preserving democratic accountability while building capacity for rapid, coordinated action on urgent challenges. Chapters 8–11 develop concrete mechanisms for achieving this balance, demonstrating that democracy need not surrender to either plutocracy or authoritarianism.

Part II

THE FRAMEWORK

3

FIVE PRINCIPLES OF DEMOCRATIC WEALTH STEWARDSHIP

FROM DIAGNOSIS TO FRAMEWORK

The preceding chapters documented twin crises: extreme wealth concentration that enables authoritarian threats through information control, policy capture, trust erosion and parallel governance (Chapter 1); and an innovation-democracy tension where rapid change, global scale and technical complexity strain democratic institutions' capacity to respond effectively (Chapter 2). These crises intersect and compound: concentrated wealth accelerates technological change beyond democratic control while democratic dysfunction creates openings for authoritarian alternatives promising speed and order.

Addressing these crises requires moving beyond diagnosis to prescription – a normative framework for governing concentrated wealth that preserves democratic accountability while enabling effective responses to urgent challenges. This chapter articulates such a framework through five interconnected principles:

Reframing Property: From Ownership to Stewardship – Reconceptualising extreme wealth as power requiring public justification rather than absolute private entitlement.

Democratic Participation: From Consultation to Meaningful Oversight – Institutionalising citizen authority over wealth accumulation and deployment, not merely soliciting input.

Intergenerational Justice: Extending Democracy Across Time – Embedding future generations' interests in present decision-making about wealth's long-term consequences.

Managing the Deliberation-Effectiveness Tension – Designing institutions that balance democratic legitimacy with the speed and expertise contemporary challenges demand.

Authoritarian Resilience and Comprehensive Accountability – Preventing concentrated wealth from being weaponised for anti-democratic purposes through transparency and structural safeguards.

These principles are interdependent: property reframed as stewardship creates conceptual space for democratic participation; meaningful participation requires intergenerational perspective to avoid short-termism; deliberation-effectiveness balance enables timely action without sacrificing legitimacy; and authoritarian resilience protections prevent wealth from capturing democratic processes. Together, they constitute a coherent vision of Democratic Wealth Stewardship – governance arrangements that treat concentrated wealth as a public trust requiring democratic authorisation rather than a private domain beyond collective accountability.

This framework differs fundamentally from conventional approaches to wealth and inequality. Standard progressive policy focuses on redistribution through taxation and social spending, treating wealth as legitimately private but excessively concentrated. Standard libertarian approaches treat wealth as inviolable property rights requiring minimal interference. The Democratic Wealth Stewardship framework rejects both: it challenges the premise that extreme wealth is simply 'private property' rather than a form of power, while acknowledging that concentrated resources – properly governed – can serve legitimate public purposes.

The framework also rejects authoritarian alternatives that sacrifice rights for efficiency or technocratic approaches that bypass democratic deliberation. It insists that democratic legitimacy is non-negotiable while recognising that democratic institutions must adapt to contemporary challenges rather than operate unchanged.

PRINCIPLE ONE: REFRAMING PROPERTY – FROM OWNERSHIP TO STEWARDSHIP

The first and most fundamental principle challenges conventional understandings of property rights. In liberal societies, property is typically conceptualised as a sphere of individual autonomy – 'mine' versus 'yours' – protected from collective interference except when necessary to prevent direct harm to others. This conception treats wealth accumulation as the product of individual effort, merit, and prudence, creating strong presumptions against redistribution or collective control.

This conventional view, however, obscures essential truths about wealth accumulation. No individual creates wealth in isolation. All accumulation depends on social infrastructure: legal systems protecting contracts and property; public education creating skilled workforces; government-funded research enabling technological innovation; transportation and communication infrastructure facilitating commerce; stable governance providing security; and accumulated knowledge – the 'shoulders of giants' – on which all innovation builds.

Consider contemporary technology fortunes. Jeff Bezos's Amazon fortune depends entirely on internet infrastructure initially developed through government-funded research (ARPANET), the World Wide Web created by publicly employed scientists and GPS systems developed by the US military, public education producing both Amazon's workforce and its customers, legal frameworks protecting intellectual property and enforcing contracts and transportation systems delivering products. Bezos's entrepreneurial vision and execution certainly contributed to Amazon's success, but the majority of preconditions were socially produced.

Similarly, pharmaceutical fortunes depend on publicly funded basic research – the National Institutes of Health spent over $40 billion annually on biomedical research by 2024, generating discoveries that private companies then commercialise (NIH, 2024). Financial fortunes depend on government stabilisation of banking systems, regulatory frameworks, and implicit bailout guarantees. Real estate wealth depends on public infrastructure, zoning decisions, and legal protections. Even 'self-made' technology entrepreneurs attended public universities, employed publicly educated workers and built on publicly funded research.

The social origins of wealth imply social obligations. If wealth accumulation is fundamentally collaborative – depending on infrastructure, institutions, knowledge and stability produced socially – then extreme wealth holders are not absolute owners but stewards of resources produced collectively. They hold wealth temporarily, with obligations to deploy it in ways serving broad public purposes rather than merely private interests.

These social origins have profoundly racialised dimensions. European wealth concentrations reflect centuries of colonial extraction – Belgian fortunes built on Congolese rubber and mineral wealth, British capital accumulated through Indian exploitation and French wealth derived from Caribbean plantation slavery and African colonialism. In the United States, white wealth accumulation systematically excluded Black Americans through slavery, Jim Crow laws, New Deal programme restrictions, GI Bill discrimination, and FHA redlining that prevented Black families from accessing homeownership wealth-building. Indigenous peoples faced land dispossession that transferred vast wealth to white settlers. The median white American family holds eight times the wealth of the median Black family – a gap rooted in these historical injustices, not individual merit differences (Federal Reserve, 2022). The stewardship principle must therefore address not only current concentration but also historical injustices embedded in wealth's origins. Democratic wealth governance requires reparative measures alongside prospective regulation, recognising that today's fortunes rest on foundations of racial exclusion and extraction.

This reconceptualisation has philosophical grounding in multiple traditions. Social contract theory, from Locke through Rawls, treats property rights as conventional arrangements justified by their contribution to collective well-being rather than natural entitlements (Locke, 1689; Rawls, 1971). Republican political theory emphasises that concentrations of private power threaten the freedom of citizens, justifying collective limits on wealth to preserve political equality (Pettit, 1997; Sandel, 1996). Capabilities approaches argue that justice requires ensuring all individuals have meaningful opportunities to pursue valuable lives, which extreme inequality systematically denies (Nussbaum, 2011; Sen, 1999).

Legal scholars Thomas Piketty and Gabriel Zucman (2014) demonstrate that property rights themselves are politically constructed and historically variable. What counts as 'property', who can own it, how it can be transferred and what obligations attach to it are all determined through collective political processes. The notion of absolute, inviolable property rights is a recent and anomalous development; throughout history, property has been understood as embedded in social relationships with attendant duties and constraints.

Political theorist Liam Murphy and philosopher Thomas Nagel (2002) make this point starkly: 'There is no such thing as pre-tax income'. All income and wealth exist only within institutional frameworks – legal systems, enforcement mechanisms, currency regimes and market regulations – that are collectively created and maintained. Claims about 'my' money being taken through taxation invert causality; the money only exists because of collective arrangements, and its distribution reflects political choices rather than natural facts.

The stewardship principle follows from these insights. If extreme wealth is:

Socially produced through infrastructure, institutions, and accumulated knowledge created collectively;

Politically constituted through legal frameworks and enforcement that are democratically determined;

Power over others' life chances, not merely private consumption;

Then wealth holders are stewards of socially produced resources, accountable to democratic communities for their deployment. This does not erase individual contribution or eliminate private property, but it contextualises wealth within social relationships and obligations.

IMPLICATIONS FOR GOVERNANCE

Reconceptualising wealth as stewardship rather than absolute ownership carries profound implications:

JUSTIFICATORY BURDEN REVERSAL

In conventional property rights frameworks, collective interference with wealth requires justification – government must demonstrate compelling reasons (externalities, market failures, rights violations) to tax or regulate. Under the stewardship framework, the burden reverses: extreme wealth accumulation and deployment require public justification. Wealth holders must demonstrate that their resource control serves legitimate purposes and does not undermine democratic institutions or future generations' well-being.

This reversal parallels how democratic societies treat other forms of concentrated power. Political authority requires justification to citizens through elections, constitutions and rights protections. Military force requires authorisation and oversight. Even property that affects public health and safety – pharmaceutical factories, nuclear facilities and food processing – faces regulatory obligations and inspection. Why should concentrated economic power, with comparable societal impacts, face less scrutiny?

PUBLIC PURPOSE REQUIREMENTS

If wealth is stewarded rather than absolutely owned, its deployment must serve public purposes, not merely private preferences. This does not mean government control of all wealth, but it does mean that tax-advantaged wealth accumulation – through preferential capital gains rates, unlimited wealth accumulation, perpetual trusts and charitable deductions – must be justified by public benefit, not donor gratification.

Current foundation law nominally includes public purpose requirements: foundations must pursue 'charitable' missions and face restrictions on political activity and self-dealing. However, definitions of 'charitable purpose' are so expansive – including elite university endowments, arts institutions serving affluent populations and ideological advocacy – that they provide minimal constraint. Moreover, foundations face no requirements for democratic accountability to affected communities, no obligations for racial equity and minimal transparency beyond basic financial disclosures.

The stewardship principle would tighten public purpose requirements substantially. Foundations controlling billions of dollars would face obligations to demonstrate how their work addresses democratically identified priorities, benefits underserved populations, incorporates affected community voices and does not perpetuate racial or economic hierarchies. Tax-advantaged wealth accumulation would require showing that concentrated resource control produces greater public benefit than alternative arrangements.

LIMITS ON DYNASTIC WEALTH

If wealth is held in stewardship rather than owned absolutely, there are principled grounds for limiting intergenerational transmission. Dynastic wealth – fortunes passed across generations through inheritance – divorces resource control from any social contribution by inheritors. Heirs did not create the wealth, do not necessarily possess competence to deploy it productively yet exercise power over others' life chances through inherited resources.

Current estate and inheritance taxation in most countries is weak and easily circumvented. In the United States, estate taxes apply only to estates exceeding $13.6 million per individual ($27.2 million for couples) as of 2024, with rates of 40% on amounts above that threshold – but aggressive tax planning through trusts, valuation manipulations and charitable vehicles enables many ultra-wealthy families to transfer billions with minimal taxation (Tax Policy Center, 2024). The result is persistent wealth dynasties: families like the Waltons, Kochs, Mars and Cargill-MacMillans have held top wealth positions for decades, perpetuating privilege across generations despite minimal social contribution by current heirs.

The stewardship principle supports substantially stronger inheritance taxation. If wealth is socially produced and held in temporary stewardship, there is limited moral basis for allowing unlimited intergenerational transfer. Inheritors might reasonably receive sufficient resources for security and opportunity – certainly more than most citizens inherit – but transfers of hundreds of millions or billions of dollars perpetuate power dynasties incompatible with democratic equality. Economists Emmanuel Saez and Gabriel Zucman (2019) propose progressive wealth taxation with higher rates on inherited wealth, recognising that inherited fortunes carry weaker justification than wealth accumulated through (socially enabled) entrepreneurship.

WORKER AND COMMUNITY VOICE

If wealth generation is collaborative – depending on workers' labour, community infrastructure, and social institutions – then workers and communities warrant a voice in how wealth is deployed. This challenges the conventional model of shareholder primacy, where corporate governance answers exclusively to capital providers.

Worker representation on corporate boards, common in German and Nordic corporate governance, reflects stewardship principles: decisions about corporate strategy, investment, and surplus distribution affect workers profoundly, justifying their participation in governance. Similarly, when corporations affect community well-being – through environmental impacts, employment levels, and tax contributions – communities warrant meaningful input rather than simply bearing externalities.

Global examples demonstrate stewardship principles in practice. Chile's 2021–2023 constitutional process included provisions for economic democracy and indigenous rights in resource governance, though ultimately rejected by voters on other grounds. Brazil's participatory budgeting – pioneered in Porto Alegre in 1989 and spreading to over 300 Brazilian municipalities – gives citizens direct authority over public spending allocation, demonstrating that ordinary people can make sophisticated resource decisions when provided genuine power (Wampler, 2007). India's social audits, mandated under the Mahatma Gandhi National Rural Employment Guarantee Act, empower village assemblies to audit public expenditures and hold officials accountable (Jenkins & Goetz, 2010). These mechanisms, while imperfect, show stewardship principles can operate across diverse contexts.

These mechanisms are elaborated in Chapters 8–10 on governance structures. The key point here is conceptual: once we recognise that wealth is socially produced and collaborative, the premise that wealth holders alone should control deployment collapses. Legitimate governance requires input from all who contribute to and are affected by concentrated resources.

PRINCIPLE TWO: DEMOCRATIC PARTICIPATION – FROM CONSULTATION TO MEANINGFUL OVERSIGHT

The second principle operationalises the first by institutionalising democratic authority over concentrated wealth. If wealth is held in stewardship with public obligations, then democratic citizens – not just wealth holders and self-selected trustees – must exercise meaningful oversight. This requires moving beyond tokenistic 'consultation' towards participatory structures with actual decision-making power.

THE CONSULTATION TRAP

Current philanthropic practice frequently includes 'community engagement' and 'stakeholder consultation' – foundation staff meet with non-profit leaders, conduct listening tours, and solicit input on priorities. While better than nothing, consultation often functions as legitimation theatre rather than genuine power-sharing. Foundations predetermine agendas, select which voices to consult, filter input through professional staff and retain unilateral decision authority. Communities provide 'input', but trustees and staff make decisions.

This dynamic reflects fundamental power asymmetries. Non-profits dependent on foundation funding face strong incentives to affirm rather than challenge foundation priorities. Community members invited to consultations understand they are guests in processes controlled by others. Even well-intentioned consultation operates within parameters foundations set:

acceptable topics, meeting formats, timeframes, and decision-making authority all remain under foundation control.

Consultation without authority amounts to what political scientist Sherry Arnstein (1969) famously termed 'tokenism' on her 'ladder of citizen participation'. Genuine participation requires actual power to shape decisions, allocates resources and holds institutions accountable. Anything less is performative democracy – legitimating elite control through participation aesthetics while preserving substantive power hierarchies.

Yet achieving these participatory structures may be more politically feasible than conventional wisdom suggests. The current moment creates distinctive openings: populist energy across the political spectrum reflects widespread frustration with elite impunity and captured governance; climate urgency generates pressure for massive public investment requiring progressive revenue sources; younger generations facing unprecedented wealth barriers show markedly greater openness to structural economic reform; and racial justice movements have foregrounded how concentrated wealth perpetuates historical injustices. These dynamics enable coalition-building among diverse constituencies – labour unions, environmental advocates, racial justice organisations, small business owners threatened by monopolistic tech platforms, and younger voters – all confronting concentrated wealth's political and economic power from different angles. Historical precedents exist: the New Deal faced similar claims of impossibility before crisis enabled transformative reform. Chapter 11 examines implementation strategies, but readers should understand democratic wealth stewardship responds to emerging political possibilities, not utopian fantasy.

MEANINGFUL OVERSIGHT REQUIREMENTS

Democratic participation in wealth governance requires institutional structures providing citizens with genuine decision-making authority. This includes the following:

Citizen Oversight Panels With Binding Authority

Major foundations – those controlling assets exceeding $1 billion or distributing more than $50 million annually – should be required to establish citizen oversight panels with binding authority over strategic priorities, major grants and policy positions. These panels would not micromanage operations but would set frameworks constraining foundation discretion, similar to how corporate boards oversee management.

Panel composition should reflect affected populations rather than elite networks. Members would be selected through random sortition from affected communities (similar to jury duty) or through elections among non-profit organisations in relevant fields, ensuring representation of grass-roots rather than just professionalised non-profit leadership. Terms would be limited to prevent capture, and members would receive compensation enabling participation by non-wealthy citizens.

Panel authority must be meaningful, not advisory. This means binding votes on overall strategic direction (e.g., foundation focuses on climate, education or health); major grants above specified thresholds (e.g., $5 million); policy advocacy positions the foundation adopts and evaluation of foundation leadership. Without binding authority, panels replicate consultation dynamics – offering legitimacy without power.

International models provide precedent. Norway's 'Framtidspanelet' (Citizens' Panel on Future Generations), established in 2023, gives randomly selected citizens authority to review major policy decisions for intergenerational impacts (Framtidspanelet, 2025). The panel issues reports that Parliament must formally consider. While still advisory rather than binding, it demonstrates institutional mechanisms for citizen input on complex, long-term challenges. Democratic wealth governance would extend this model to a binding authority.

Participatory Grantmaking

Beyond strategic oversight, democratic participation should extend to resource allocation decisions. Participatory grantmaking – where community members directly decide which organisations receive funding – has emerged as a practice in a small but growing number of foundations. The Disability Rights Fund, Wellspring Philanthropic Fund's participatory initiatives, and the Marginalised Community Grantmaking programme have demonstrated that community-led allocation can identify effective organisations, build civic capacity and distribute resources more equitably than traditional philanthropy (Participatory Grantmaking Community, 2024).

Research on participatory budgeting – where citizens directly allocate portions of public budgets – provides evidence of effectiveness. Across over 3,000 cities globally practicing participatory budgeting, studies find improved service delivery, reduced corruption, increased civic engagement and more equitable resource distribution compared to traditional budgeting (Baiocchi, 2005; Wampler et al., 2019). Meta-analyses show that participatory processes do not degrade efficiency or decision quality; indeed, they often improve outcomes by incorporating local knowledge and building accountability (Sintomer et al., 2013).

Participatory grantmaking would operate through structured processes: communities identify priorities through deliberation; organisations apply for funding; community panels (compensated for their time) review applications; deliberative sessions assess proposals; and community members vote on allocations. Foundation staff provide technical support, facilitate deliberation and implement decisions, but allocation authority rests with citizens rather than professional programme officers.

Worker Voice in Corporate Governance

Wealth accumulation increasingly occurs through corporate ownership rather than individual entrepreneurship. Amazon's, Apple's and Microsoft's market capitalisations exceed $2–3 trillion each – wealth nominally belonging to shareholders but fundamentally depending on workers' labour and collective effort. Democratic participation requires worker voice in corporate governance, not just shareholder primacy.

Worker representation on corporate boards, standard in German 'Mitbestimmung' (codetermination) and widespread across Northern Europe, provides meaningful participation in strategic decisions about investment, compensation, production location and labour relations (Hagen, 2020). Research shows that worker representation does not reduce firm performance – German firms with board-level worker representation are as profitable as comparable firms without it – while improving working conditions, reducing inequality and stabilising employment (Jäger et al., 2021).

US Senator Elizabeth Warren's 'Accountable Capitalism Act', proposed in 2018 and reintroduced in 2023, would require large corporations (revenue exceeding $1 billion) to allocate 40% of board seats to worker-elected directors, mirroring German codetermination (Warren, 2018). This would democratise governance of immense concentrations of economic power – the 500 largest US corporations represent over $40 trillion in market capitalisation and employ over 28 million workers (S&P 500 Index, 2024).

Worker participation need not be limited to boards. Works councils – elected worker committees with consultation rights and limited veto power over major decisions – provide additional participatory structures. Employee stock ownership plans (ESOPs), when structured to provide genuine voting rights rather than just financial stakes, can democratise ownership. The key is ensuring that those who create wealth through labour have a voice in governance, not just those who own capital.

COMMUNITY BENEFIT AGREEMENTS

When corporations or foundations make investments significantly affecting communities – building facilities, funding development projects and initiating programmes – communities should negotiate binding benefit agreements specifying employment, environmental and social obligations. These agreements recognise that 'development' affects existing residents, not just investors or philanthropists, and that affected communities warrant authority over terms.

Community benefit agreements (CBAs) have been negotiated for major real estate developments, sports facilities and corporate relocations in cities across the United States. For example, the 2001 Figueroa Corridor Coalition agreement in Los Angeles secured commitments for living-wage jobs, affordable housing and local hiring from a major downtown development (Gross, 2008). The Atlantic Yards CBA in Brooklyn committed the developer to affordable housing, job training and park space (Been, 2010). While CBAs vary in enforcement strength, they demonstrate institutional mechanisms for community authority over development affecting local residents.

Extending this model to philanthropic investments would require foundations undertaking major place-based initiatives – say, a $100 million education or community development programme – to negotiate binding agreements with community representatives specifying priorities, accountability mechanisms and evaluation criteria. Communities would have authority to reject initiatives that do not meet their needs or to demand modifications aligning with local priorities.

DELIBERATIVE DEMOCRATIC THEORY

These participatory mechanisms draw on deliberative democratic theory, which emphasises reasoned discussion among citizens as central to legitimate governance (Cohen, 1997; Gutmann & Thompson, 2004; Habermas, 1996). Deliberative democrats argue that legitimate decisions require not just aggregating preferences through voting but also engaging in reasoned exchange where participants offer justifications, consider alternative perspectives, and potentially revise views based on better arguments.

Political scientist James Fishkin's (2018) research on 'deliberative polling' demonstrates that structured deliberation transforms citizen thinking. When randomly selected citizens receive balanced information, engage in facilitated discussion and hear from diverse experts, they develop more sophisticated, coherent policy preferences that often differ substantially from their initial views. Importantly, this deliberation does not produce uniform agreement – citizens still disagree – but disagreements become more informed and reasoned.

Wealth governance benefits particularly from deliberative processes because distributional questions involve competing values and interests. Should foundations prioritise education or health? Direct service or advocacy? Domestic or international? Immediate relief or long-term prevention? There are no purely 'technical' answers – these are value-laden choices requiring democratic deliberation rather than expert determination.

Empirical research on deliberative democracy shows positive effects. Citizens participating in deliberative processes report increased political efficacy, trust in institutions and civic engagement (Gastil et al., 2010). Deliberative participants become more tolerant of opposing views and more willing to compromise (Fishkin, 2018). Policies emerging from deliberation enjoy greater public legitimacy, even among those who disagree with outcomes, because the process itself is perceived as fair (Esaiasson et al., 2019).

ADDRESSING OBJECTIONS

Critics raise several objections to democratising wealth governance:

- 'Ordinary Citizens Lack Expertise'
  This objection assumes that wealth governance primarily requires technical expertise rather than value judgements. While some decisions involve technical complexity – evaluating medical research proposals, assessing financial risk – most foundational choices are normative: What problems warrant priority? Whose needs matter most? What constitutes success? These questions require democratic judgement, not just expert knowledge. Moreover, research on citizen deliberation shows that ordinary people, when provided with information and opportunities for deliberation, make

thoughtful decisions on complex matters (Landemore, 2012). Juries routinely evaluate complex evidence in criminal and civil trials. Citizen assemblies addressing climate policy, healthcare reform and constitutional questions have produced sophisticated recommendations (Farrell et al., 2019). The 'expertise' objection often reflects the elite assumption that ordinary citizens are incapable of reasoned judgement – an assumption empirical evidence refutes.

Where genuine technical expertise is required, participatory structures can incorporate expert input while retaining citizen authority over fundamental choices. Experts provide information, analysis and implementation guidance, but citizens determine values and priorities. This mirrors how elected officials rely on expert civil servants while retaining political authority.

- 'Participation Is Inefficient'
  Deliberation and participation take time, potentially slowing decision-making. However, 'efficiency' is not the only or even primary value in governance. Legitimate decisions – those that affected parties view as fair – often require time-consuming deliberation. Moreover, participation can improve long-term efficiency by identifying problems experts overlook, building buy-in that facilitates implementation and preventing costly mistakes.

  Research on participatory budgeting shows that participatory processes do not substantially slow decision-making and often improve outcomes by incorporating local knowledge (Baiocchi, 2005; Wampler et al., 2019). When citizens identify infrastructure priorities, for example, they often select projects delivering greater community benefit than technocrats would choose, because they understand local needs directly.

  Chapter 3's fourth principle addresses deliberation-effectiveness balance, proposing institutional designs that enable timely action while preserving meaningful participation. The key insight is that participation and effectiveness are not necessarily in tension; properly designed processes can achieve both.

- 'Capture by Special Interests'
  Sceptics worry that participatory processes will be captured by organised interest groups or vocal minorities, producing outcomes skewed towards those with time and resources to participate. This is a real concern: public comment processes are often dominated by narrow interests, homeowner associations capture land-use decisions, and well-organised groups can overwhelm disorganised majorities.

However, these risks can be mitigated through careful institutional design. Random sortition – selecting participants through lottery – ensures broad representation rather than self-selection. Compensation for participation enables inclusion of working-class and marginalised citizens who cannot afford volunteer time. Facilitation by trained moderators prevents domination by vocal individuals. And binding authority distributed across many participants reduces any single group's ability to capture outcomes.

Moreover, current wealth governance is already captured – by wealth holders themselves and elite networks they select as trustees. Democratisation does not introduce capture risk; it redistributes power from one group (economic elites) to the broader citizenry. The question is not whether capture occurs but whose interests governance serves.

PRINCIPLE THREE: INTERGENERATIONAL JUSTICE – EXTENDING DEMOCRACY ACROSS TIME

Democratic participation, as described above, operates primarily in the present: current citizens exercise authority over current decisions. However, concentrated wealth's impacts often extend decades or centuries into the future. Climate change, biodiversity loss, technological trajectories and foundational research investments shape conditions for generations not yet born. Principle Three addresses this temporal dimension: how can democratic governance incorporate future generations' interests when they cannot participate directly?

THE PROBLEM OF FUTURE GENERATIONS

Future people face a political representation problem: they cannot vote, deliberate or protest. Yet present decisions profoundly affect their well-being. Greenhouse gas emissions today determine climate conditions decades hence. Species extinctions today eliminate biodiversity permanently. Foundation endowments establish priorities that persist across generations. Debt accumulation shifts costs to future taxpayers. Property rights and legal frameworks structure future opportunity sets.

The philosopher Derek Parfit (1984) illuminated this problem through thought experiments showing that present actions affecting future people raise distinctive ethical challenges. We can predictably benefit or harm billions of future people, yet standard ethical and political frameworks operate primarily within generations. Democracy assumes coexistence: citizens negotiate arrangements governing mutual relations. But future people are excluded from this negotiation, creating systematic bias towards present interests.

This temporal bias appears starkly in climate politics. Mitigation requires present costs (carbon taxes, fossil fuel restrictions, infrastructure investment) to prevent future harms (catastrophic warming, sea level rise, ecosystem collapse). Yet democratic electoral cycles spanning 2–6 years create incentives to defer costs while harvesting immediate political benefits. Politicians win elections by promising tax cuts and economic growth today, not by imposing sacrifices for climate stability in 2050.

Similarly, foundation perpetuity creates intergenerational impacts. When billionaires establish foundations with instructions to exist 'in perpetuity', they embed their values across centuries. The Ford Foundation, established in 1936, continues operating according to founder Henry Ford's (subsequently modified) vision 88 years later. The Carnegie Corporation, founded in 1911, persists 113 years after Andrew Carnegie's death. These institutions govern resources across multiple human generations according to founders' long-dead preferences – hardly democratic governance.

PHILOSOPHICAL FOUNDATIONS

Several philosophical traditions support intergenerational obligations:

Intergenerational Justice Theories

Philosopher John Rawls (1971) argued that justice requires ensuring fair conditions for future generations. His 'just savings principle' obligates each generation to preserve and improve social institutions, accumulate capital, and maintain environmental conditions enabling successive generations to enjoy justice. Rawls explicitly rejected preference utilitarianism across generations – simply aggregating present and future interests – in favour of a principle requiring each generation to act as trustee for the next.

Building on Rawls, philosophers like Axel Gosseries (2008) and Samuel Scheffler (2018) elaborate principles of intergenerational justice. Gosseries distinguishes 'sufficiency' principles (ensuring each generation has sufficient resources) from 'equality' principles (ensuring comparable resources across generations) and 'priority' principles (prioritising worse-off generations).

Scheffler argues that concern for future generations is central to human motivation and meaning – we act for purposes extending beyond our lifetimes precisely because we care about post-mortem futures.

Sustainability and Environmental Ethics

Environmental ethicists argue that present generations hold Earth's ecosystems in trust for future inhabitants. The World Commission on Environment and Development (1987) defined sustainable development as 'meeting the needs of the present without compromising the ability of future generations to meet their own needs' – making future capacity preservation a defining constraint on present action. Philosopher Hans Jonas (1984) proposed a 'principle of responsibility' requiring present actors to consider long-term consequences and avoid actions foreclosing future options.

These principles find expression in legal doctrines like the 'public trust doctrine', which treats certain resources (navigable waters, wildlife, atmosphere) as held in trust for future generations with present governments as trustees obligated to preserve them. Several countries have constitutionalised intergenerational rights: Article 20a of Germany's Basic Law requires the state to protect natural life foundations 'in responsibility for future generations'. Ecuador's 2008 Constitution recognises nature's rights and intergenerational equity. The Philippines Supreme Court ruled in *Oposa v. Factoran* (1993) that citizens could sue to protect forests on behalf of unborn generations.

Republican Freedom Across Time

Republican political theory emphasises non-domination – freedom as non-subjection to arbitrary power (Pettit, 1997). Intergenerational domination occurs when present generations exercise arbitrary power over future people's life prospects without constraint. Climate change represents domination: present populations impose catastrophic conditions on future people who have no recourse.

Similarly, permanent foundations exercise intergenerational domination. When a billionaire establishes a foundation to exist in perpetuity, implementing their values across centuries, they exercise power over future generations who cannot challenge or revise those priorities. This violates republican principles requiring that power be contestable by those subject to it.

INSTITUTIONAL MECHANISMS

Incorporating future generations' interests requires institutional innovation, translating abstract principles into concrete governance:

Future Generations Commissioners

Several countries have established officials or institutions specifically charged with representing future interests. Hungary's Commissioner for Future Generations (2008–2011) reviewed legislation for long-term impacts. Wales's Future Generations Commissioner, established in 2015, ensures public bodies consider long-term well-being in decisions. Israel's Commission for Future Generations (2001–2006) advised Parliament on intergenerational implications of legislation (Pettit, 1997).

Norway's Framtidspanelet (Citizens' Panel on Future Generations), established in 2023, randomly selects citizens to review major policy decisions for impacts on future well-being (Framtidspanelet, 2025). The panel issues reports Parliament must formally consider, creating institutional space for long-term thinking.

Applied to wealth governance, future generations' commissioners could review foundation endowment policies, evaluate investment strategies for sustainability, assess programme priorities for long-term impacts and recommend modifications serving intergenerational equity. Commissioners would lack veto power but would create an institutional voice for future interests in present deliberation.

Sunset Provisions for Perpetual Institutions

Rather than allowing foundations to exist indefinitely according to founders' frozen preferences, democratic governance could require periodic renewal or sunset provisions. Foundations might be chartered for fixed terms (e.g., 25 years) requiring stakeholder approval for renewal. This would force periodic re-evaluation: do current priorities serve contemporary needs? Should governance structures be reformed? Should assets be spent down or continue accumulating?

Some philanthropists have embraced this approach voluntarily. The Atlantic Philanthropies, established by billionaire Chuck Feeney, deliberately spent down its $8 billion endowment by 2020 rather than operating in perpetuity (Bill & Melinda Gates Foundation, 2022). The Bill & Melinda Gates Foundation plans to spend its endowment within 20 years of the deaths of its founders (Forbes, 2017). These 'giving while living' or 'spend-down' approaches recognise that founder preferences should not dominate indefinitely and that present deployment may serve greater social benefit than perpetual accumulation.

Sunset provisions could be structured flexibly: foundations demonstrating ongoing social benefit and democratic accountability through citizen oversight mechanisms could receive renewal; those failing to demonstrate contemporary relevance would dissolve, with assets redistributed according to democratic processes.

Long-Term Investment Requirements

If foundations exist across generations, their investment strategies should reflect intergenerational obligations. Current foundation practice often prioritises maximising returns to sustain perpetual operations, investing in portfolios that may generate negative social or environmental externalities. Foundations routinely hold fossil fuel investments, private prison stocks, weapons manufacturers and companies with poor labour practices – generating returns through activities contradicting their charitable missions.

Intergenerational justice requires aligning investments with long-term well-being. Foundations should divest from industries imposing costs on future generations (fossil fuels, unsustainable extraction) and invest in sectors supporting long-term flourishing (renewable energy, sustainable agriculture, education, health). This 'mission-aligned investing' treats the endowment itself as a tool for social benefit rather than merely a funding source.

Several foundations have adopted this approach. The Nathan Cummings Foundation divested from fossil fuels and invested in clean energy (Nathan Cummings Foundation, 2020). The Heron Foundation invests 100% of its assets – not just grants – for mission (Heron Foundation, 2024). These models demonstrate the feasibility of integrating intergenerational obligations into investment practice.

Climate Trust Funds

Addressing climate change requires mobilising concentrated wealth for long-term mitigation and adaptation. Climate trust funds – permanent pools of capital dedicated to climate action – provide institutional mechanisms. Norway's Government Pension Fund Global, capitalised by oil revenues, exceeds $1.4 trillion and increasingly directs investment towards climate solutions (Norway Government Pension Fund, 2024). Green investment banks in several countries leverage public and philanthropic capital for climate infrastructure.

Democratic wealth governance could require ultra-wealthy individuals and corporations to contribute to intergenerational climate trust funds as a condition for tax-advantaged wealth accumulation. These funds would operate under democratic oversight with mandates to serve future generations' climate security. By pooling resources and operating across decades, trust funds overcome individual foundations' limitations while embedding intergenerational obligations.

Youth and Future-Oriented Quotas

Intergenerational representation can be enhanced by ensuring that young people – whose futures are longest – participate meaningfully in wealth governance. Foundation oversight panels could include reserved seats for citizens under 30. Corporate boards could include youth representatives. Deliberative processes could employ stratified sampling, ensuring age diversity.

Some jurisdictions have lowered voting ages for certain decisions. Scotland allowed 16-year-olds to vote in the 2014 independence referendum, recognising that constitutional decisions profoundly affect young people's futures (Electoral Commission, 2014). Austria, Brazil and Argentina allow 16-year-olds to vote in national elections. Extending this logic, decisions about long-lived institutions and intergenerational impacts warrant youth participation.

Addressing Short-Termism

These mechanisms address but do not eliminate democratic short-termism – the tendency for elected governments and citizens to prioritise immediate interests over long-term well-being. Several additional approaches can mitigate temporal bias:

Enforceable Long-Term Targets: Legally binding emissions reduction targets, biodiversity protection goals and debt limits constrain present discretion to impose costs on future generations.

Independent Monitoring and Transparency: Regular public reporting on progress towards long-term goals creates accountability for intergenerational obligations.

Constitutional Protections: Enshrining intergenerational rights in constitutional law insulates them from ordinary political pressures, as Germany's constitutional provision for future generations' protection demonstrates.

Educational and Cultural Shifts: Cultivating intergenerational consciousness through education, media and cultural narratives can shift public priorities towards long-term thinking.

The fourth principle, managing the deliberation-effectiveness tension, further addresses how democratic institutions can balance present urgency with intergenerational responsibility.

PRINCIPLE FOUR: MANAGING THE DELIBERATION-EFFECTIVENESS TENSION

The innovation-democracy tension documented in Chapter 2 poses a fundamental governance challenge: how can democratic institutions respond effectively to rapid change, global scale and technical complexity without sacrificing the deliberation, accountability and rights protections that define legitimate governance? Principle Four addresses this tension through institutional designs that balance democratic participation with timely, expert-informed action.

THE DUAL IMPERATIVE

Democratic legitimacy and effective response are both non-negotiable values. Legitimacy requires that those affected by decisions have a meaningful voice in making them – participation, deliberation and accountability are not merely instrumental to good outcomes but constitutive of respecting persons as free and equal. Effectiveness requires that governance institutions can act with sufficient speed, scale and expertise to address urgent challenges – climate stabilisation, pandemic response, AI safety and financial stability.

The challenge is that legitimacy and effectiveness can pull in opposite directions. Deliberation takes time; crises demand rapid response. Democratic participation involves broad inclusion; technical decisions require specialised expertise. Accountability mechanisms create procedural constraints; urgent action requires flexibility. Electoral cycles operate in years; technological change occurs in months.

However, this tension is not absolute. Properly designed institutions can achieve both legitimacy and effectiveness by:

distributing authority appropriately between democratic bodies (setting values and priorities) and expert institutions (implementing technical decisions within democratic constraints);

creating tiered deliberation where routine decisions follow streamlined processes while consequential choices receive fuller democratic engagement;

embedding accountability through transparency, monitoring and retrospective review rather than solely through prior authorisation;

institutionalising expertise within democratic frameworks rather than delegating authority to technocrats insulated from accountability.

Institutional Design Strategies

Democratic Constraint on Expert Implementation

Many decisions involve both normative choices (what goals to pursue, whose interests to prioritise) and technical judgements (how to achieve goals efficiently). Legitimacy requires democratic authority over normative choices; effectiveness benefits from expert judgement on implementation.

This suggests a division of authority: democratic bodies set binding constraints reflecting public values, while expert institutions exercise discretion within those constraints. Central bank independence illustrates this model imperfectly: legislatures establish mandates (price stability, maximum employment) and appoint officials, while insulated central bankers determine technical implementation (interest rates, reserve requirements, asset purchases).

Applied to wealth governance, democratic citizen oversight panels (Principle Two) would establish strategic frameworks constraining foundation discretion: priority populations (e.g., lowest-income 40%, communities of colour); priority issues (e.g., climate, health, education); geographic scope (e.g., 50% resources to local communities); and prohibited activities (e.g., no funding organisations violating labour rights). Within these democratically determined constraints, foundation professionals exercise expertise selecting specific grantees, designing programmes and evaluating outcomes.

This differs from current practice, where foundation boards – typically composed of wealthy trustees and hand-selected experts – establish both normative priorities and implementation strategies without democratic input. Democratic constraint rebalances authority: citizens determine 'what for' and 'for whom', while experts determine 'how'.

TIERED DELIBERATION

Not all decisions warrant equal deliberative investment. Routine operational choices – hiring staff, renewing existing grants, maintaining facilities – can follow streamlined processes. Strategic decisions with long-term implications – establishing new programme areas, making multi-million dollar commitments, adopting policy positions – warrant intensive deliberation with broad participation.

Tiered deliberation establishes thresholds triggering different processes. For example:

Tier 1 (Routine): Grants under $500,000, operational decisions → Staff discretion with periodic reporting to oversight panels.

Tier 2 (Significant): Grants $500,000–$5 million, programme modifications → Oversight panel review and approval.

Tier 3 (Strategic): Grants exceeding $5 million, new programme areas, major policy positions → Full citizen deliberation involving affected communities, expert input and public comment.

This approach balances efficiency (avoiding deliberative paralysis on routine matters) with legitimacy (ensuring meaningful participation on consequential choices). Thresholds can be calibrated to institutional scale: larger foundations with greater social impact face lower thresholds for triggering intensive deliberation.

CONTINGENT EMERGENCY POWERS WITH RETROSPECTIVE REVIEW

Genuine emergencies – pandemics, natural disasters, financial crises and immediate humanitarian needs – may require rapid response, precluding extensive prior deliberation. Democratic governance can accommodate urgency through contingent emergency powers: pre-authorised authority to act quickly in specified circumstances, subject to retrospective democratic review.

This model parallels constitutional emergency provisions: executives receive temporary expanded authority during crises but face requirements to justify actions to legislatures and courts after the fact. Applied to wealth governance, foundations could receive authorisation to make rapid large grants during declared emergencies (natural disasters, pandemics, acute humanitarian crises) without prior oversight panel approval, but would face mandatory retrospective review within specified timeframes (e.g., 60 days).

Retrospective review assesses whether emergency criteria genuinely applied; responses served stated emergency purposes; expenditures were reasonable; and affected communities' interests were considered. If the review reveals that emergency powers were misused, oversight panels could impose sanctions (leadership changes, restricted future discretion, financial penalties).

This design enables rapid response without sacrificing accountability. The possibility of retrospective sanction incentivises responsible emergency decision-making even absent prior approval. And democratic communities retain ultimate authority – emergency powers are delegated conditionally, not surrendered permanently.

STRUCTURED EXPERT INPUT WITHIN DEMOCRATIC PROCESSES

Democratic deliberation need not exclude expertise; indeed, informed deliberation requires expert input. The challenge is structuring expert participation to inform rather than dominate democratic judgement.

Deliberative democracy scholars propose several mechanisms:

Expert Panels With Diverse Perspectives: Rather than single 'authoritative' experts, include multiple experts with different viewpoints, making contestation among experts visible to citizen deliberators.

Facilitated Expert Testimony: Experts present findings in accessible language, respond to citizen questions and explicitly distinguish technical judgements from value choices.

Citizen Review of Expert Reasoning: Citizens evaluate not just expert conclusions but the reasoning supporting them, learning to assess evidence quality and identify assumptions.

Adversarial Collaboration: Experts with opposing views jointly present findings, highlighting consensus areas and clarifying genuine disagreements (Mellers et al., 2014).

These approaches avoid two extremes: technocracy (experts decide without democratic input) and populism (rejecting expertise entirely). Instead, they integrate expert knowledge into processes where citizens retain decision authority.

Research on science courts, consensus conferences and citizen juries demonstrates that ordinary citizens can evaluate expert testimony, ask probing questions and reach sophisticated judgements on technical matters (Kleinman et al., 2017). Citizens do not become experts themselves but develop sufficient understanding to make informed normative choices.

TRANSPARENCY AND REAL-TIME MONITORING

When rapid action precludes extensive prior deliberation, real-time transparency and monitoring enable ongoing accountability. Digital technologies make it feasible to provide public access to decision-making as it unfolds: streaming meetings, publishing drafts, sharing data and soliciting continuous feedback.

Foundations could operate 'open by default': all meetings open to public observation (except where privacy genuinely requires confidentiality), all grant applications and decisions published, all evaluation data shared and all strategic deliberations documented publicly. This radical transparency enables affected communities to monitor foundation activities, raise concerns and demand course corrections without waiting for formal review cycles.

Several governments have experimented with participatory real-time monitoring. Taiwan's Digital Ministry uses online platforms where citizens propose policies, debate alternatives and monitor implementation. Iceland's constitutional revision process (2011–2013) operated through crowdsourced input and transparent drafting (Landemore, 2015). While these experiments have limitations, they demonstrate institutional possibilities for combining speed with democratic oversight.

EMPIRICAL EVIDENCE ON DELIBERATION AND EFFECTIVENESS

Critics argue that deliberation inherently slows decision-making and degrades quality. However, empirical research challenges this assumption:

Participatory Budgeting Efficiency

Studies of participatory budgeting across thousands of cities find no systematic evidence that participation reduces efficiency. Indeed, research in Brazil, Peru and Italy shows that participatory budgeting often improves resource allocation by incorporating local knowledge about priorities and implementation feasibility (Baiocchi, 2005; Wampler et al., 2019). While participatory processes take more time initially, they reduce implementation delays by building buy-in and identifying potential problems early.

Deliberation Improves Policy Quality

Political scientist Helene Landemore's (2012) research demonstrates that diverse groups of ordinary citizens often outperform expert groups on complex problem-solving because cognitive diversity generates more comprehensive analysis and creative solutions. This 'diversity trumps ability' finding suggests that deliberative processes incorporating varied perspectives produce better decisions than technocratic processes relying on homogeneous expert opinion.

Democratic Legitimacy Facilitates Implementation

Policies developed through deliberative processes enjoy greater public legitimacy, facilitating implementation and reducing resistance. Research on renewable energy siting shows that projects developed with meaningful community participation face less opposition and proceed more smoothly than projects imposed by technocratic planning (Fast & Mabee, 2015). The time invested in deliberation is recovered through smoother implementation.

Trade-offs Are Real but Manageable

Some research does find trade-offs between deliberation and speed. Political scientists Knill and Steinbacher (2021) show that transparency requirements can slow EU decision-making. However, they find these delays are modest (weeks, not years) and that combining transparency with flexibility in implementation maintains effectiveness while improving legitimacy.

The key insight is that deliberation-effectiveness tensions are institutional design challenges, not inherent contradictions. Well-designed institutions can achieve both values, while poorly designed institutions sacrifice both (ineffective because illegitimate, illegitimate because bypassing participation).

The Authoritarian Efficiency Myth

Addressing deliberation-effectiveness tension is crucial because authoritarian movements exploit perceived democratic inefficiency to justify concentrated power. However, claims of authoritarian efficiency rest on selective examples and ignore systematic failures.

China's rapid infrastructure development is frequently cited, but this overlooks massive resource misallocation: ghost cities, underutilised high-speed rail, unsustainable debt levels and environmental destruction. China's authoritarian system lacks error-correction mechanisms, allowing failed policies to persist because critics are silenced. The initial COVID-19 cover-up – local officials suppressing information to avoid admitting problems, enabling the outbreak to spread globally – illustrates how authoritarian systems' apparent efficiency masks catastrophic vulnerabilities.

Research by political scientists Daron Acemoglu and James Robinson (2012) demonstrates that autocracies systematically underperform democracies in long-run economic growth, innovation and social development precisely because they lack democratic accountability that identifies and corrects mistakes. Authoritarian regimes may achieve short-term mobilisation, but democratic institutions enable sustained prosperity by incorporating feedback, protecting rights that foster innovation and preventing extractive policies.

Democratic institutions that balance deliberation with effectiveness avoid false choices between rights and results, demonstrating that legitimate governance can be effective governance.

PRINCIPLE FIVE: AUTHORITARIAN RESILIENCE AND COMPREHENSIVE ACCOUNTABILITY

The final principle addresses how concentrated wealth can be prevented from undermining democracy itself. As Chapter 1 documented, extreme wealth enables authoritarian threats through information control, policy capture, trust erosion, parallel governance and surveillance infrastructure. Principle Five establishes institutional safeguards ensuring that concentrated wealth, even when serving legitimate public purposes, cannot be weaponised against democratic institutions.

The Dual Challenge

Democratic wealth stewardship faces a paradox: concentrated resources are needed to address urgent challenges at scale (climate change, pandemic preparedness, technological governance), yet concentration itself threatens democracy. The solution cannot be simply eliminating all wealth concentration – that would sacrifice potential benefits and might be politically unachievable. Instead, governance must enable resource mobilisation while preventing anti-democratic weaponisation.

This requires two complementary strategies:

Structural Safeguards: Institutional designs preventing wealth concentration from translating into political domination, information control or parallel governance beyond democratic accountability.

Comprehensive Transparency and Accountability: Mechanisms ensuring that wealth deployment remains visible to democratic publics and subject to ongoing scrutiny, enabling citizens to identify and address anti-democratic uses.

Structural Safeguards

Prohibitions on Media Ownership by Major Wealth Holders

As discussed in Chapter 1, billionaire ownership of major media institutions creates profound informational power. Jeff Bezos's ownership of The Washington Post, Rupert Murdoch's News Corp empire and similar concentrations grant wealthy individuals outsized influence over public discourse (Repucci & Slipowitz, 2021).

Democratic resilience requires limiting such ownership. Several democracies restrict media concentration: limits on ownership across multiple platforms (broadcast, print, digital), restrictions on foreign ownership and prohibitions on cross-ownership of media and other industries with regulatory interests. These could be extended to prohibit individuals or entities controlling wealth exceeding specified thresholds from owning major media institutions.

Alternatively, major media institutions could be required to convert to public benefit corporations, worker cooperatives or trust structures preventing individual control. The Guardian newspaper operates under trust ownership, insulating editorial independence from commercial pressures (Guardian Media Group, 2024). Public broadcasting models (BBC, NPR, PBS) demonstrate that high-quality journalism can operate without billionaire ownership. Germany's media diversity requirements prevent concentration, maintaining pluralistic information ecosystems (Puppis et al., 2016).

PLATFORM GOVERNANCE AND ALGORITHMIC ACCOUNTABILITY

Digital platforms – Meta's social networks, Google's search and YouTube and Amazon's marketplace – exercise unprecedented informational power through algorithms determining what billions of users see. Democratic resilience requires bringing platform governance under democratic accountability.

Proposals include the following:

Algorithmic Transparency Requirements: Platforms must disclose how algorithms prioritise content, enabling independent auditing.

Democratic Oversight Boards: Citizen panels with binding authority review content moderation policies, algorithmic designs, and platform governance decisions.

Interoperability Requirements: Users can migrate data and social connections across platforms, reducing lock-in and dominant platform power.

Prohibition on Surveillance Business Models: Ban data harvesting and microtargeting practices that enable manipulative advertising and political interference.

The EU's Digital Services Act (2022) and Digital Markets Act (2023) represent steps towards democratic platform governance, establishing transparency requirements, content moderation oversight and constraints on dominant platforms (European Commission, 2022). However, implementation remains limited, and stronger measures – including democratic oversight boards with authority over algorithmic design – are necessary to prevent platform power from undermining democracy.

CAMPAIGN FINANCE AND LOBBYING LIMITS

Policy capture through campaign contributions and lobbying systematically advantages wealthy interests. Democratic resilience requires constraining money's political influence.

Reforms include the following:

Public Campaign Financing: Provide sufficient public funding so that candidates need not depend on wealthy donors. Models include small-donor matching (New York City's 8:1 match amplifying grassroots contributions), voucher systems (Seattle's democracy vouchers giving each voter $100 to allocate to candidates) and full public financing (several states' Clean Elections systems).

Contribution Limits and Disclosure: Strengthen individual contribution limits, close Super PAC loopholes and require real-time disclosure of all contributions above minimal thresholds.

Lobbying Restrictions: Limit lobbying expenditures, establish cooling-off periods preventing government officials from becoming lobbyists, require disclosure of all lobbying contacts and restrict former legislators from lobbying.

Shareholder Protection: Require shareholder approval for corporate political expenditures, preventing executives from using corporate resources for political purposes without owner consent.

These reforms would not eliminate wealth's political influence entirely, but they would substantially reduce plutocratic domination. Research by political scientists Joshua Kalla and David Broockman (2016) shows that lobbying influence operates primarily through access and information provision; constraining both reduces wealthy interests' systematic advantages.

ANTITRUST ENFORCEMENT PREVENTING POLITICAL POWER ACCUMULATION

Economic concentration translates into political power: dominant firms can threaten to relocate, withhold investment or fund opposition if governments enact unfavourable policies. Vigorous antitrust enforcement prevents economic power from reaching levels that enable political capture.

The US antitrust tradition historically recognised this political dimension. Supreme Court Justice Louis Brandeis warned that 'we may have democracy, or we may have wealth concentrated in the hands of a few, but we can't have both' (Brandeis, 1941). The Sherman Anti-Trust Act (1890) and Clayton Act (1914) aimed not just at economic efficiency but at dispersing power. However, since the 1970s, antitrust enforcement has focused narrowly on consumer welfare and pricing, ignoring political concentration.

The emerging 'neo-Brandeis' approach returns to political considerations. Legal scholar Lina Khan argues that dominant platforms like Amazon exercise monopoly power beyond traditional price effects, controlling market access, data flows and innovation trajectories (Khan, 2017). Breaking up or regulating dominant firms based on political power criteria – not just economic efficiency – would reduce concentrated wealth's capacity to dominate governance.

PROHIBITIONS ON PARALLEL GOVERNANCE

As discussed under Principle Two, large foundations function as parallel governance structures making public priority decisions without democratic authorisation. Democratic resilience requires constraining this parallel governance through the following:

Mandatory citizen oversight panels with binding authority over foundation strategies (already discussed).

Limits on foundation political advocacy: Foundations can fund research and service delivery but face strict limits on lobbying and electoral activity.

Sunset provisions: Foundations charter for fixed terms requiring democratic renewal rather than existing in perpetuity.

Restrictions on founder control: Limit founders' ability to dictate foundation priorities decades after death, requiring periodic democratic revisiting of missions.

These mechanisms prevent wealthy individuals from establishing permanent institutions implementing their values across generations without democratic accountability.

COMPREHENSIVE TRANSPARENCY AND ACCOUNTABILITY

Even with structural safeguards, concentrated wealth requires ongoing democratic monitoring. Transparency makes power visible; accountability enables correction when power is misused.

Beneficial Ownership Registries

Wealthy individuals often hide asset ownership through shell companies, trusts, and offshore entities, making it impossible to trace wealth's influence. Beneficial ownership registries require disclosure of ultimate owners behind corporate and financial structures, enabling public and journalistic scrutiny.

The United Kingdom established a beneficial ownership registry in 2016, requiring companies to disclose 'persons with significant control' (Companies House, 2024). The EU's Anti-Money Laundering Directives require member states to maintain beneficial ownership registries. However, enforcement remains weak, and many jurisdictions – particularly tax havens – maintain secrecy. Comprehensive transparency requires:

Global Coordination: International agreements requiring beneficial ownership disclosure across all jurisdictions, with sanctions for non-compliance.

Public Access: Registries accessible to journalists, civil society and researchers, not just law enforcement.

Real-Time Updating: Ownership changes are reported immediately, not annually.

Trust Transparency: Extension to trusts and other wealth-holding vehicles, not just corporations.

Foundation and Non-profit Transparency

Current foundation disclosure – IRS Form 990 in the United States – provides minimal information: total revenues, expenditures and largest grants. This is insufficient for democratic accountability.

Enhanced transparency would require:

Detailed Grant Information: All grants above minimal thresholds ($10,000) disclosed with recipient, purpose, amount and term.

Investment Portfolio Disclosure: Complete holdings disclosed quarterly, enabling scrutiny of whether investments align with the mission.

Influence Disclosure: All contacts with government officials, testimony, policy advocacy and political activities disclosed.

Evaluation Data: Outcomes assessment and evaluation data made public, enabling independent analysis of effectiveness.

Compensation Disclosure: All employee and contractor compensation above thresholds disclosed, revealing insider benefits.

The United Kingdom's Charity Commission requires more extensive disclosure than US law, including detailed annual reports and accessible financial statements (Charity Commission, 2024). However, even UK requirements fall short of the comprehensive transparency necessary for democratic accountability.

Political Spending and Lobbying Transparency

All lobbying activities and political expenditures by wealthy individuals, corporations and foundations should be disclosed in real-time public databases. This includes the following:

Campaign Contributions: All contributions disclosed within 48 hours.

Independent Expenditures: Super PAC and dark money spending disclosed immediately with donor identification.

Lobbying Contacts: All meetings between lobbyists and government officials logged publicly.

Revolving Door Tracking: Public database of officials entering lobbying and lobbyists entering government, enabling conflict-of-interest monitoring.

ALGORITHMIC TRANSPARENCY AND AUDIT RIGHTS

Platform algorithms shaping information flows must be subject to an independent audit. This requires the following:

Algorithm Disclosure: Platform companies provide algorithm specifications to independent auditors.

Audit Rights: Regulators and independent researchers can test algorithms with real data.

Impact Assessments: Platforms must conduct and publish assessments of algorithmic impacts on polarisation, misinformation and democratic discourse.

User Transparency: Users receive explanations of why content is recommended or suppressed.

These measures make platform power visible and contestable rather than hidden in proprietary systems.

Whistle-blower Protections and Independent Journalism

Transparency requirements only work if violations are detected and reported. This requires:

Strong Whistle-blower Protections: Legal safeguards and financial rewards for individuals exposing wrongdoing in foundations, corporations and government.

Independent Investigative Journalism: Public funding for investigative journalism focused on wealth and power, since ad-supported commercial media often avoid scrutinising wealthy interests.

Civil Society Capacity: Resources for watchdog organisations monitoring foundation activities, corporate political influence and government-wealth interactions.

The International Consortium of Investigative Journalists (2016, 2021) demonstrated investigative journalism's power to expose wealth's hidden structures. Sustaining such capacity requires institutional support recognising journalism's democratic function.

ENFORCEMENT AND SANCTIONS

Transparency and safeguards require enforcement. Violations must carry meaningful consequences:

Financial Penalties: Substantial fines for disclosure violations, scaled to violator resources (percentage of wealth/assets rather than fixed amounts).

Criminal Liability: Personal criminal penalties for executives and trustees knowingly violating democratic safeguards.

Charter Revocation: Foundations or corporations persistently violating democratic governance requirements lose tax-exempt status or corporate charters.

Disqualification: Individuals convicted of serious violations face disqualification from corporate or foundation leadership.

These sanctions ensure that democratic resilience protections have teeth rather than operating as aspirational guidelines.

4

HISTORICAL LESSONS

Understanding contemporary wealth concentration and democratic governance benefits from a historical perspective. Extreme wealth concentration and its political consequences are not new; earlier eras provide lessons about both dangers and potential responses. This chapter briefly examines two historical cases illustrating wealth's political power and attempts at democratic control: the Fugger banking dynasty in Renaissance Europe and Alfred Nobel's creation of the Nobel Prizes.

THE FUGGER BANKING DYNASTY: WEALTH AS POLITICAL POWER

Historical wealth governance efforts span diverse contexts beyond the United States. Norway's Government Pension Fund Global – commonly called the Oil Fund – exemplifies democratic stewardship of resource wealth. Established in 1990, the fund invests Norway's petroleum revenues for future generations rather than allowing immediate consumption or private capture. Managed according to parliamentary oversight, ethical investment guidelines and transparency requirements, the fund held over $1.4 trillion by 2024 – approximately $250,000 per Norwegian citizen (Norges Bank Investment Management, 2024). Its success demonstrates that democratic institutions can steward concentrated wealth effectively across generations.

Sweden's Meidner Plan, proposed in 1976, would have gradually transferred corporate ownership to worker-controlled funds through profit-based levies, democratising Sweden's concentrated capital over decades. Though ultimately defeated by employer opposition and capital flight threats, the Meidner Plan demonstrated labour movements' capacity to develop sophisticated wealth governance alternatives (Pontusson, 1987). West Germany's postwar codetermination laws required worker representation on corporate supervisory boards, democratising governance of concentrated industrial capital. Japan's postwar land reform redistributed agricultural wealth from large landowners to tenant farmers, dramatically reducing wealth concentration while enabling agricultural productivity growth (Dore, 1959). These international examples show that wealth governance reforms succeeded across varied institutional contexts when political conditions aligned.

The Fugger family of Augsburg exemplifies how extreme wealth concentration translates into political power, even in pre-democratic contexts. At their peak in the early 16th century, the Fuggers operated Europe's largest financial enterprise, controlling mining operations, trading networks and lending to monarchs across the continent.

WEALTH ACCUMULATION AND POLITICAL INFLUENCE

Jakob Fugger (1459–1525), known as "Jakob the Rich," built the family fortune through textile trade, mining ventures in silver and copper and financial services. By the 1520s, Fugger's wealth was estimated at 2% of European GDP, equivalent to over $400 billion today (Häberlein, 2012). This concentration gave the Fuggers extraordinary political leverage.

The Fuggers' most consequential political intervention came in 1519, when they financed Charles V's election as Holy Roman Emperor. Charles required massive bribes to secure electors' support and Fugger loans totalling 851,000 florins (approximately $100 million today) proved decisive (Ehrenberg, 1928). In exchange, the Fuggers received mining rights, tax farming privileges and monopolistic control over copper and silver trade. They effectively purchased imperial power, demonstrating wealth's capacity to determine political outcomes.

The Fuggers also financed papal activities, including the infamous indulgence sales that partially funded the construction of St. Peter's Basilica. Johann Tetzel's aggressive indulgence selling – "as soon as a coin in the coffer rings, a soul from purgatory springs" – provoked Martin Luther's protest in 1517, sparking the Protestant Reformation (MacCulloch, 2003). Thus, Fugger's financial interests inadvertently contributed to the most significant religious-political transformation in European history.

DEMOCRATIC LESSONS

The Fugger case illustrates several enduring patterns:

Wealth Buys Political Power: The Fuggers purchased an imperial election, demonstrating that concentrated wealth enables the direct capture of political authority.

Economic and Political Power Reinforce Each Other: Imperial favour granted the Fuggers monopolistic advantages, generating more wealth that funded further political influence – a self-reinforcing cycle.

Accountability Gaps Enable Abuse: The Fuggers operated without democratic oversight, answering only to family interests. Their pursuit of profit destabilised papal authority and inadvertently triggered religious warfare.

Eventually, Overreach Invites Backlash: Fugger monopolies and political manipulation generated resentment. When Spanish King Charles V (the same Charles whose election they financed) defaulted on loans in 1557, the Fuggers faced financial ruin. Their concentrated power proved brittle when political circumstances shifted.

The Fugger case reminds us that extreme wealth concentration creates governance challenges even in non-democratic systems. In democracies, where political equality is a foundational principle, such concentration poses even greater legitimacy problems.

ALFRED NOBEL: REDEMPTIVE PHILANTHROPY AND DONOR CONTROL

Alfred Nobel's (1833–1896) establishment of the Nobel Prizes illustrates both the potential and problems of using private wealth for public purposes. Nobel, a Swedish chemist and industrialist, invented dynamite and accumulated a massive fortune through explosives manufacturing. His will, written in 1895, dedicated his wealth to annual prizes recognising outstanding contributions to physics, chemistry, physiology or medicine, literature and peace.

MOTIVATIONS AND IMPLEMENTATION

Nobel reportedly established the prizes partly out of guilt over dynamite's military applications and partly out of a desire for a posthumous legacy. His will specified detailed criteria: prizes should go to those conferring "the greatest benefit to humankind" in the preceding year. He appointed the Royal Swedish Academy of Sciences, the Swedish Academy, the Karolinska Institute and the Norwegian Parliament to administer prize selections in various categories.

The Nobel Prizes have become extraordinarily influential, shaping scientific research priorities, literary canons and peace activism for over a century. Nobel laureates gain global recognition, institutional positions and amplified platforms. The prizes direct attention and resources towards Nobel-validated fields and approaches.

DEMOCRATIC GOVERNANCE ISSUES

However, the Nobel Prizes also illustrate philanthropic governance problems:

Donor Control Persisting Posthumously: Nobel's will, written in 1895, continues to govern prize criteria 130 years later. Contemporary society has no mechanism to revise Nobel's priorities – his values, determined in the 19th century, permanently shape 21st-century recognition.

Critically, US New Deal reforms systematically excluded Black Americans, limiting their transformative potential and embedding racial hierarchies in new programmes. The GI Bill provided education and housing benefits, enabling white wealth accumulation, but excluded many Black veterans through discriminatory administration. FHA mortgage insurance explicitly promoted redlining, refusing loans in Black neighbourhoods and concentrating public housing benefits in white suburbs. Agricultural programmes excluded sharecroppers and tenant farmers, who were disproportionately Black (Katznelson, 2005). These racialised exclusions created durable wealth gaps and taught essential lessons: contemporary democratic wealth stewardship must centre racial justice from inception, not as an afterthought, to avoid replicating historical failures that deepened rather than remedied racial inequalities.

Narrow Elite Composition: Prize-awarding bodies are self-perpetuating elite institutions – royal academies and universities – without democratic input from affected global communities. The Nobel Peace Prize has been controversial (Henry Kissinger in 1973, Aung San Suu Kyi in 1991 – later involved in genocide, Barack Obama in 2009 just months into his presidency), demonstrating how elite judgement can diverge from broader democratic values.

Structural Biases: Nobel Prizes have systematically underrepresented women, people of colour and scholars from the Global South. Only 64 out of 954 Nobel laureates through 2023 were women, representing just 6.7% (Nobel Foundation, 2024). No African scientist working in Africa has won a Nobel Prize in science. These patterns reflect institutional biases in elite prize-awarding bodies.

Disciplinary Limitations: Nobel's 1895 will could not anticipate 21st-century challenges. There are no Nobel Prizes for climate science, computer science, environmental conservation, or human rights – fields crucial to contemporary wellbeing but excluded by 19th-century categories.

No Democratic Accountability: When Nobel decisions prove controversial – as with multiple Peace Prize selections – there is no mechanism for affected publics to contest them or reform governance. The prize-awarding institutions answer only to themselves.

ALTERNATIVE MODELS

The Nobel case suggests that philanthropic institutions governing significant resources should have mechanisms for democratic revision. Rather than permanent donor control, prizes and foundations could:

Include sunset provisions: Automatically expire after specified periods (e.g. 50 years), requiring affirmative democratic renewal.

Build in revision mechanisms: Allow periodic democratic review and updating of priorities.

Establish democratic oversight: Include citizen panels with authority to modify criteria and governance.

Ensure representative composition: Require prize-awarding bodies to include diverse demographic and geographic representation.

Some newer prizes incorporate these features. The Right Livelihood Award (established 1980), sometimes called the "Alternative Nobel Prize," explicitly includes Global South representation and periodically revisits criteria (Right Livelihood Foundation, 2024). The Breakthrough Prizes (established 2013), while still donor-controlled, include more diverse selection committees than traditional Nobel bodies.

CONTEMPORARY IMPLICATIONS

These historical cases – separated by four centuries – reveal persistent patterns:

Wealth and Political Power Are Inextricable: From Renaissance banking dynasties to contemporary tech billionaires, concentrated wealth enables political influence through financing, access and leverage over economic systems. Democratic governance must constrain this transformation of economic power into political power.

Philanthropic Intent Alone Is Insufficient: Nobel established prizes for admirable purposes, yet governance problems such as lack of accountability, demographic bias and frozen priorities – persist. Good intentions do not guarantee democratic legitimacy.

Concentration Creates Brittleness: The Fuggers' concentrated power proved vulnerable to shifting political winds. Contemporary mega-foundations face similar risks: when public opinion turns against elite philanthropy or when economic crises diminish endowments, their power proves less stable than it appears.

Democratic Oversight Requires Institutionalisation: Neither the Fuggers nor Nobel faced systematic democratic accountability. Contemporary democratic wealth stewardship must institutionalise oversight mechanisms – citizen panels, transparency requirements, periodic renewal – rather than rely on voluntary elite responsibility.

Learning and Adaptation Are Essential: Nobel's 1895 categories cannot address 2025 challenges. Governance institutions must incorporate learning and adaptation rather than freezing priorities across generations. This requires democratic mechanisms for revision, not permanent donor control.

These lessons inform the concrete policy proposals developed in Part IV. History demonstrates both the urgency of democratic wealth governance and the feasibility of institutional designs constraining concentrated power while enabling resource mobilisation for public purposes.

Part III

THE DUAL NATURE

5

WHEN PRIVATE WEALTH SERVES PUBLIC GOOD

The preceding chapters emphasised threats that concentrated wealth poses to democracy. However, a comprehensive analysis must acknowledge that private wealth, when properly deployed, can generate significant public benefits. This chapter examines three prominent cases where concentrated private resources have advanced public purposes: the Bill & Melinda Gates Foundation's global health work, Bloomberg Philanthropies' climate action and Patagonia's stakeholder capitalism model. These cases illuminate both the potential benefits and persistent democratic deficits of private wealth deployment.

GLOBAL HEALTH: THE GATES FOUNDATION'S TRANSFORMATIVE IMPACT

Yet acknowledging philanthropic successes does not establish that billionaire control is necessary for achievement. The Gates Foundation's malaria interventions show concentrated wealth can fund valuable work, but the World Health Organization and member states eradicated smallpox without billionaire philanthropy – through coordinated public action (Fenner et al., 1988). Taiwan's semiconductor leadership developed through government-funded research consortia (ITRI, TSMC's origins), not private fortunes. Israeli agricultural innovation emerged substantially through kibbutz collective structures combining shared ownership with research investment. Postwar Europe achieved extraordinary public health and infrastructure advances despite much higher wealth taxation than contemporary levels. The Scandinavian countries lead global innovation indices while maintaining robust wealth redistribution.

The question is not whether concentrated wealth can fund beneficial activities – clearly it can – but whether benefits require concentrated *control* versus adequate resources under more democratic governance. Innovation and effective problem-solving require sufficient funding, technical capacity, risk tolerance and long-time horizons. Democratic institutions can provide these through progressive taxation, funding robust public investment. The innovation argument for billionaire wealth conflates resource adequacy (necessary) with concentrated private control (not demonstrated as necessary).

The Bill & Melinda Gates Foundation, with over $70 billion in assets, represents the largest private foundation in history (Bill & Melinda Gates Foundation, 2024). Its global health programmes have achieved measurable improvements in disease prevention, treatment access and health infrastructure across low- and middle-income countries.

ACHIEVEMENTS AND SCALE

The foundation's most significant contributions include the following:

Vaccine Development and Delivery: Gates Foundation funding accelerated development and distribution of vaccines for rotavirus, pneumococcus and HPV in low-income countries. The foundation's support for Gavi, the Vaccine Alliance (over $4 billion through 2023), enabled vaccination of over 1 billion children, preventing an estimated 17 million deaths (Gavi, 2024). During COVID-19, the foundation committed $2 billion to vaccine development, manufacturing and equitable distribution, supporting successful vaccines and financing delivery infrastructure.

Malaria Control: The foundation has invested over $2 billion in malaria research and control since 2000. This funding supported the development of new antimalarial drugs, insecticide-treated bed nets, rapid diagnostic tests and vector control strategies. Global malaria deaths declined from 736,000 in 2000 to 608,000 in 2022 – a 17% reduction despite population growth – with Gates-funded interventions contributing significantly (WHO, 2023).

Polio Eradication: Gates Foundation funding (over $5 billion total) was instrumental in driving polio towards eradication. In 1988, polio paralysed 350,000 children annually across 125 countries; by 2023, only 12 wild poliovirus cases were reported, all in Pakistan and Afghanistan (Global Polio Eradication Initiative, 2024). The foundation's strategic focus, technical support and political advocacy sustained momentum when government commitment wavered.

Health Systems Strengthening: Beyond specific diseases, the foundation invested in health workforce training, supply chain management, data systems and primary care infrastructure in sub-Saharan Africa and South Asia. These investments built capacity, enabling broader health improvements beyond foundation-prioritised diseases.

Credible estimates attribute 6–10 million lives saved to Gates Foundation-funded interventions over two decades (Jamison et al., 2013; Evaluation Office, Bill & Melinda Gates Foundation, 2022). This represents one of the most consequential health interventions by any organisation, public or private, in modern history.

DEMOCRATIC DEFICITS

Despite these achievements, the Gates Foundation's operations illustrate persistent democratic governance problems:

Agenda-Setting Power: The foundation's resource scale enables it to define global health priorities. When Gates emphasises vaccines and technical interventions over health systems strengthening or addressing social determinants of health, this shapes where the global health community directs attention and resources. Critics argue that the foundation's focus on technological solutions reflects Western biomedical assumptions rather than holistic approaches to health that communities might prioritise (Birn, 2014; McGoey, 2015).

Influence Over International Organizations: The foundation's funding – providing approximately 12% of WHO's budget by 2023 – grants it substantial influence over WHO priorities, research agendas and programme implementation (WHO, 2023). Some critics describe WHO as partially captured by Gates' interests, implementing foundation priorities rather than priorities that member states or affected populations would determine democratically (Storeng, 2014).

Lack of Community Voice: While the foundation consults extensively with governments, NGOs and technical experts, affected communities have minimal direct voice in priority-setting. Decisions about which diseases to target, which interventions to fund and how programmes are implemented are made in Seattle by foundation staff and trustees, not through participatory processes involving those affected.

Accountability Gaps: When foundation initiatives underperform or cause unintended harms, there is no democratic accountability mechanism. The foundation's failed investments in for-profit pharmaceutical companies that subsequently raised prices, its support for intellectual property protections that delayed generic drug access and its promotion of controversial agricultural technologies in Africa all occurred without accountability to affected populations (Schwab Foundation, 2020).

Perpetuating Dependency: By financing significant portions of global health infrastructure, the foundation creates dependency: when Gates' priorities shift, countries and organisations dependent on funding must adapt or face resource loss. This shifts governance from democratic states accountable to citizens towards a private foundation accountable to donors.

CLIMATE ACTION: BLOOMBERG PHILANTHROPIES' BEYOND COAL CAMPAIGN

Michael Bloomberg's climate philanthropy, channelled through Bloomberg Philanthropies, demonstrates how private wealth can accelerate policy change in gridlocked political systems. The Beyond Coal campaign, launched in 2011, aimed to retire all US coal-fired power plants by 2030.

ACHIEVEMENTS

By 2024, the campaign contributed to retiring 373 of the 530 US coal plants operating in 2010 – a 70% reduction (Sierra Club, 2024). This accelerated coal's decline beyond market forces alone, achieving emissions reductions equivalent to approximately 1 billion tons of CO_2 avoided cumulatively through 2024 (Bloomberg Philanthropies, 2024).

The campaign's strategies included the following:

Litigation and Regulatory Advocacy: Funding environmental organisations challenging coal plant permits, advocating for stricter EPA regulations and supporting state-level renewable energy standards.

Local Coalition Building: Supporting grassroots groups organising communities affected by coal pollution to demand plant retirements and transition planning.

Economic Analysis: Commissioning research demonstrating that renewable energy plus storage was cost-competitive with existing coal plants, undermining utilities' economic justifications for coal continuation.

Utility Engagement: Direct engagement with utility executives, offering transition assistance and demonstrating renewable pathways.

These tactics proved effective where legislative action stalled: despite Congressional gridlock on climate policy, Beyond Coal achieved tangible emissions reductions through administrative, legal and economic pressure.

DEMOCRATIC CONCERNS

However, the campaign also raises governance questions:

Billionaire Policy Dominance: Bloomberg's personal climate priorities – emphasising coal retirement over other interventions – dominated US environmental advocacy during the 2010s because his resources dwarfed those of other actors. Whether coal retirement was the optimal climate priority (versus transportation electrification, building efficiency, land use reform or adaptation) was determined by one billionaire's judgement, not democratic deliberation.

Strategic Limitations: The campaign focused on coal plant closures without adequately addressing just transitions for affected workers and communities. Coal-dependent regions experienced economic devastation as plants closed, contributing to political backlash and support for climate-sceptical politicians. Democratic processes might have better balanced emissions reduction with worker and community needs (Haggerty et al., 2018).

Tactical Controversies: Some criticised the campaign's aggressive litigation tactics as bypassing democratic processes. When courts and regulators made climate policy in response to advocacy funded by a billionaire, this arguably substituted judicial/administrative governance for legislative deliberation that might better balance competing interests.

Accountability Absence: Bloomberg's philanthropy faces no requirement to consider equity impacts, engage affected communities democratically or revise strategies based on community input. His personal vision shaped US climate policy significantly without democratic authorisation.

CORPORATE INNOVATION: PATAGONIA'S STAKEHOLDER CAPITALISM

Patagonia, the outdoor apparel company founded by Yvon Chouinard, exemplifies how corporate wealth can be structured to serve broad stakeholder interests rather than solely shareholder profit maximisation. In September 2022, Chouinard transferred company ownership (valued at approximately $3 billion) to a trust and nonprofit structure, ensuring that all profits beyond operational reinvestment go towards environmental protection (Patagonia, 2022).

MODEL FEATURES

Patagonia's governance includes the following:

Environmental Mission Priority: The company's charter explicitly prioritises environmental sustainability over profit maximisation. Business decisions consider ecological impacts systematically, with practices including organic materials, supply chain transparency, repair programmes encouraging product longevity and 'don't buy this jacket' advertising campaigns discouraging overconsumption.

Worker Treatment: Patagonia provides above-market wages, comprehensive benefits, on-site childcare, flextime and encourages activism. The company famously bailed out employees arrested for environmental protests, demonstrating commitment to worker dignity beyond mere compensation.

Supply Chain Responsibility: Patagonia maintains detailed supply chain monitoring for labour conditions, environmental practices and fair wages. The company publishes its factory list and audit results, enabling external accountability.

Ownership Structure Preventing Extraction: By transferring ownership to a trust (Patagonia Purpose Trust, holding voting shares) and nonprofit (Holdfast Collective, receiving profits), Chouinard ensured that wealth generated by the company serves environmental purposes rather than personal or dynastic enrichment.

This model demonstrates that corporate wealth accumulation can be structured to serve public purposes – environmental protection, worker wellbeing, sustainable consumption – rather than simply maximising returns to capital.

LIMITATIONS AND QUESTIONS

Nevertheless, even this exemplary model faces democratic limitations:

Founder Discretion: Chouinard unilaterally determined that environmental protection should be the beneficiary of Patagonia's wealth. While this choice is laudable, it was his personal decision, not one made democratically by workers, communities or society. Alternative uses – direct wealth redistribution, worker ownership, community investment – were not considered through democratic processes.

No Worker Governance: Despite excellent treatment, Patagonia workers do not have formal governance authority. The company remains hierarchically managed, with workers as employees rather than co-owners or co-governors. Worker cooperatives like Mondragon in Spain demonstrate more democratic corporate governance models.

Limited Replicability: Patagonia's model depends on founder ideology and private company status. Publicly traded corporations face shareholder pressure for profit maximisation, making Patagonia's approach difficult to replicate at scale without legal reforms requiring stakeholder governance.

Philanthropic Control: The Holdfast Collective nonprofit receiving Patagonia's profits will make grantmaking decisions – determining which environmental organisations and causes to fund – without democratic accountability to affected communities. This replicates traditional foundation governance problems despite admirable intent.

SYNTHESIS: POTENTIAL AND DEFICITS

These three cases demonstrate that concentrated private wealth can generate significant public benefits:

Speed and Risk-Taking: Private actors can move faster than governments and take risks that bureaucratic institutions avoid. Gates Foundation vaccine investments and Bloomberg's aggressive coal campaign achieved results unlikely through conventional policy processes.

Innovation and Experimentation: Private wealth enables testing approaches that democratically risk-averse institutions might not attempt. Patagonia's business model experiments with sustainable capitalism at scales informing broader reform.

Resource Mobilisation: Concentrated wealth provides the scale necessary for major initiatives. The Gates Foundation's $70 billion endowment enables sustained multi-decade commitments that annual government appropriations cannot match.

Technical Expertise: Large foundations and corporations can hire world-class expertise, convene diverse stakeholders and synthesise knowledge across domains more flexibly than government agencies constrained by civil service rules.

However, all three cases also exhibit persistent democratic deficits:

Lack of Democratic Authorisation: Priorities are determined by wealthy individuals or trustees they appoint, not through democratic processes involving those affected.

Accountability Gaps: When initiatives fail or cause harm, there is no electoral accountability, no democratic correction mechanism and often no systematic learning or course adjustment.

Community Voice Absence: While foundations and corporations consult stakeholders, consultation is not genuine participation with decision-making authority. Affected communities receive at most advisory roles.

Distributional Blindness: Private wealth initiatives often inadequately consider equity and justice dimensions. Efficiency and impact metrics dominate, while distributional questions – who benefits, who bears costs and how to ensure fair treatment – receive insufficient attention.

Philanthropic resource flows perpetuate racial inequalities even when addressing social problems. Research by found that Black-led nonprofit organisations receive substantially less funding than white-led organisations doing comparable work, face more restrictive grants with burdensome reporting requirements and encounter systematic bias in evaluation. Foundation 'overhead' restrictions – limiting funds for organisational infrastructure – disproportionately harm organisations led by people of colour, which typically operate with fewer reserves and less access to complementary revenue sources.

MacKenzie Scott's philanthropic approach contrasts with traditional gatekeeping by providing large, unrestricted grants to organisations led by communities most affected by issues addressed, particularly BIPOC-led groups (Scott, 2021). This highlights how stewardship principles – centring affected community authority, trusting organisational leadership, providing flexible resources – can operate even within current philanthropic structures. Democratic wealth governance would institutionalise these practices as obligations rather than depending on individual donors' enlightenment, ensuring all philanthropic deployment incorporates racial equity accountability.

These deficits underscore that even exemplary private wealth deployment requires democratic governance reforms detailed in Part IV. Private wealth's potential can be realised while addressing democratic deficits through citizen oversight, participatory mechanisms and comprehensive transparency requirements.

6

THE DEMOCRACY DEFICIT

While Chapter 5 examined private wealth's public benefits, this chapter systematically analyses democratic deficits in contemporary philanthropic practice. These deficits are not incidental flaws but structural features of private wealth governance requiring institutional reform. The analysis is organised around five interrelated problems: transparency failures, accountability gaps, participation exclusion, ideology over evidence and dependency traps.

TRANSPARENCY FAILURES IN PHILANTHROPIC PRACTICE

Democratic accountability requires that power be visible: citizens must know who exercises authority, how decisions are made, what resources are deployed and what outcomes result. Philanthropic practice systematically fails these transparency requirements.

DISCLOSURE INADEQUACY

US foundations face minimal disclosure obligations. IRS Form 990 requires reporting of total revenues, expenses, assets and compensation for key employees, plus identification of grants exceeding $5,000. However, this leaves vast information gaps:

Strategic Priorities and Decision Criteria: Foundations need not explain why they choose particular focus areas or how they determine which organisations to fund.

Rejected Applications: No disclosure of what requests were denied or why, making it impossible to assess whether allocation processes are fair.

Investment Portfolios: Limited disclosure of endowment investments, obscuring whether foundations' assets are deployed consistently with stated missions.

Evaluation Methodologies and Results: No requirement to share how effectiveness is assessed or what evaluations reveal, preventing independent quality assessment.

Political Influence Activities: Minimal reporting of lobbying, policy advocacy and political relationships that shape governance.

Research by the Foundation Center (2024) found that fewer than 15% of large US foundations (assets exceeding $100 million) voluntarily publish detailed strategic plans, and fewer than 8% publish comprehensive evaluation findings. Most foundations operate behind closed doors, making decisions affecting millions of people without public visibility into reasoning or evidence.

INTERNATIONAL OPACITY

Transparency problems intensify internationally. When US foundations operate in low- and middle-income countries – as Gates Foundation, Ford Foundation, Open Society Foundations and others do extensively – disclosure to affected populations is even weaker. Reports are typically written in English, published on US websites and framed for US audiences. Communities in sub-Saharan Africa or South Asia affected by foundation programmes often cannot access information about decision-making, fund flows or evaluation results.

Some foundations impose confidentiality requirements on grantees, preventing funded organisations from disclosing grant terms, evaluation processes or foundation feedback. This gag-like arrangement protects foundation's reputation while silencing grantees who might otherwise provide accountability through public information sharing.

These transparency deficits extend beyond US-Global South dynamics. In India, where corporate foundations control assets exceeding $3 billion, disclosure requirements remain minimal despite the Companies Act 2013 mandating 2% of profits for CSR activities. The Tata Trusts and Reliance Foundation deploy hundreds of millions annually with limited public reporting on decision criteria or evaluation results. Similarly, European foundations operating across borders – such as Germany's Bertelsmann Stiftung ($1.2 billion assets) or the UK's Wellcome Trust ($38 billion) – face inconsistent disclosure requirements depending on jurisdiction. When Swedish foundations fund development projects in East Africa or Japanese corporate foundations support education in Southeast Asia, affected communities often lack access to information about strategic priorities, funding decisions or performance assessments, replicating the accountability deficits identified in US foundation practice (Foundation Center, 2024).

DONOR-ADVISED FUND SECRECY

Donor-advised funds (DAFs), holding over $250 billion by 2024, face even less transparency than private foundations (National Philanthropic Trust, 2024). DAFs allow donors to take immediate tax deductions while retaining control over grant timing and recipients. Yet DAF sponsors (Fidelity Charitable, Schwab Charitable and community foundations) face no requirements to disclose:

Who Controls Specific DAF Accounts: Donors can remain anonymous indefinitely.

What Grants Are Made: Unlike foundations, DAFs need not report individual grants publicly.

When Funds Will Be Distributed: DAFs face minimal distribution requirements (sponsors must meet 5% payout, but individual accounts need not), enabling indefinite warehousing of tax-deducted wealth.

This opacity makes it impossible to assess whether DAFs serve public purposes justifying tax deductions or simply function as private wealth management vehicles with public subsidy.

ACCOUNTABILITY GAPS: WHEN DONORS CONTROL OUTCOMES

Democratic accountability means that those who exercise power must justify their actions to those affected and face consequences when performance fails expectations. Philanthropic governance systematically lacks such accountability.

TRUSTEE SELF-DEALING AND INSIDER BENEFIT

Foundation trustees – typically appointed by donors or self-perpetuating boards – face minimal accountability to affected communities. Research by the National Committee for Responsive Philanthropy (2020) found the following:

Homogeneous Trustee Composition: Foundation boards are overwhelmingly white (90%), wealthy (median net worth $15 million) and drawn from business/finance backgrounds (68%), reflecting elite networks rather than communities served.

Conflicts of Interest: Trustees routinely have business interests aligned with foundation funding priorities, creating conflicts. For example, education foundation trustees often have investments in education technology companies that receive foundation grants.

Family Control: Family foundations – comprising 60% of all US foundations – often function as vehicles for dynastic control, with trustees drawn exclusively from founding families across multiple generations.

Legal prohibitions on 'self-dealing' prevent blatant personal enrichment but permit subtler benefits: prestige, network access, influence and values propagation. Trustees enjoy substantial power – governing billions of dollars affecting millions of lives – without democratic authorisation or accountability.

FAILED INITIATIVE CONSEQUENCES

When foundation initiatives fail, consequences are borne by communities, not foundations. Consider the following:

Small Schools Initiative: The Gates Foundation invested over $2 billion between 2000–2010, promoting small high schools as a solution to educational inequality. Evaluations showed the initiative largely failed to improve outcomes, yet the costs – disrupted schools, displaced educators, wasted resources – were borne by communities while the foundation simply shifted priorities (Cavanagh, 2014).

Agricultural Development (AGRA): The Gates Foundation's Alliance for a Green Revolution in Africa (AGRA), launched in 2006 with over $1 billion in funding, aimed to double yields and incomes for 30 million farming households by 2020. An independent evaluation found that AGRA failed to achieve its targets; the number of undernourished people in AGRA's 13 focus countries increased by 30% during the initiative. Yet the foundation faced no accountability to African farmers for this failure.

Democratic governments face electoral consequences for failed policies; philanthropic foundations simply move on to new initiatives, leaving affected communities to cope with disruption.

NO REMEDY FOR AFFECTED PARTIES

When foundation programmes cause harm – displacing communities, disrupting service delivery, promoting ineffective interventions – affected parties have no recourse. There is no electoral mechanism to remove foundation leadership, no judicial remedy for policy mistakes and no requirement that foundations compensate for damages caused by failed experiments.

This one-way accountability – foundations judge grantees, but no one judges foundations – inverts democratic principles. In democracy, power flows from citizens to representatives who remain accountable; in philanthropy, power flows from donors to trustees who are accountable only to themselves.

THE PARTICIPATION PROBLEM: COMMUNITIES WITHOUT VOICE

As discussed in Chapter 3's second principle, genuine democratic participation requires decision-making authority, not merely consultation. Philanthropic practice systematically excludes affected communities from meaningful participation.

CONSULTATION THEATRE

Many foundations engage in 'community engagement' processes: listening tours, stakeholder meetings, advisory committees and feedback sessions. However, these typically function as legitimation mechanisms rather than genuine power-sharing.

Research by the Philanthropic Initiative for Racial Equity (2019) analysed community engagement practices at 50 large foundations and found:

Predetermined Agendas: Foundations decide priorities before 'consulting' communities, then seek input within predetermined frameworks.

Selective Inclusion: Foundations choose which community voices to hear, typically privileging professionalised nonprofit leaders over grassroots activists or affected individuals.

Advisory-Only Authority: Community input is advisory; trustees and staff retain unilateral decision authority.

No Feedback Loops: Foundations rarely explain how community input influenced decisions or why suggestions were rejected.

This consultative approach provides legitimacy benefits for foundations – demonstrating 'community engagement' – without ceding actual power.

PARTICIPATORY GRANTMAKING'S RARITY

Genuine participatory grantmaking, where community members exercise binding authority over resource allocation, remains rare. The Participatory Grantmaking Community (2024) estimates that participatory approaches account for less than 2% of total foundation giving in the United States. Most foundations retain professional staff control over all allocation decisions.

Where participatory grantmaking exists, it tends to be limited to small grants programmes (under $1 million annually) or pilot initiatives, while large strategic investments remain under centralised control. This bifurcation treats community participation as appropriate only for 'small' decisions while reserving 'important' choices for elites.

Notable international exceptions demonstrate participatory grantmaking's viability across contexts. Brazil's Fundo Baobá para Equidade Racial allocates resources through participatory processes where Afro-Brazilian community members exercise binding authority over grants supporting racial equity initiatives. In South Africa, the DG Murray Trust has implemented participatory mechanisms enabling communities affected by education and child welfare programmes to shape strategic priorities and evaluate outcomes. The Kenya Community Development Foundation practices participatory budgeting, where rural communities decide resource allocation for local development projects. These models demonstrate that participatory approaches can operate across diverse governance contexts. Yet they remain exceptions: globally, participatory grantmaking accounts for less than 3% of foundation giving, with most resources controlled by boards drawn from economic and political elites rather than affected communities.

EXCLUSION OF MARGINALISED VOICES

Even when foundations attempt community engagement, processes systematically exclude marginalised populations:

Language Barriers: Meetings conducted in English exclude non-English speakers.

Time Requirements: Uncompensated participation privileges those with flexible schedules, excluding working-class individuals.

Geographic Concentration: Foundation events in major cities exclude rural communities.

Educational Assumptions: Processes requiring literacy, formal presentation skills or technical knowledge exclude those with less formal education.

Cultural Norms: Western meeting formats and decision-making styles disadvantage communities with different deliberative traditions.

Research by the Marguerite Casey Foundation (2021) on its Equal Voice for America's Families initiative found that achieving genuine inclusion of low-income families and communities of colour required: compensation for participation time, childcare provision, multilingual facilitation, flexible meeting formats, relationship-building over extended periods and explicit power-sharing commitments. Few foundations make these investments.

IDEOLOGY OVER EVIDENCE: HOW DONOR PREFERENCES SHAPE INTERVENTIONS

Foundations frequently allow donor ideology to override evidence about effectiveness and community needs. This reflects accountability structures: foundations answer to donors, not communities served or evidence about impact.

IDEOLOGICALLY DRIVEN GRANTMAKING

Conservative foundations like the Bradley Foundation, Scaife Foundations and Donors Trust explicitly fund right-wing ideological projects: climate denial, anti-union campaigns, opposition to social safety nets and promotion of 'free market' policies (Mayer, 2016). Progressive foundations like Open Society Foundations, Ford Foundation and Atlantic Philanthropies fund left-leaning causes: criminal justice reform, immigration rights, climate action and social justice organising.

While donors have rights to political views, philanthropic practice enables tax-subsidised promotion of partisan ideologies as 'charitable' activity. The public subsidises (through tax deductions) promotion of views that might not emerge from democratic deliberation. Foundations essentially launder political preferences through charitable apparatus, gaining legitimacy and tax advantages while advancing partisan agendas.

EVIDENCE-FREE EDUCATION REFORM

Education philanthropy illustrates ideology-driven grantmaking. Despite extensive research showing that poverty, housing instability and community disinvestment are primary drivers of educational inequality (Reardon, 2011; Rothstein, 2004), foundations have overwhelmingly funded supply-side interventions – charter schools, teacher evaluation, testing – reflecting market-oriented ideologies rather than evidence about root causes (Reckhow, 2013).

The Gates Foundation's promotion of charter schools, Teach for America and Common Core State Standards occurred despite limited evidence of effectiveness and substantial community opposition (Barkan, 2018; Schneider, 2015). These initiatives reflected Bill Gates's personal beliefs about education rather than research consensus or community preferences.

PERPETUATING RACIAL HIERARCHY THROUGH FUNDING CHOICES

Foundation funding systematically advantages white-led organisations over those led by people of colour, even when serving similar populations. Research by the Bridgespan Group (2020) found that nonprofits led by people of colour receive significantly less funding than white-led organisations:

Organisations led by people of colour received 76 cents for every dollar received by white-led organisations serving similar populations.

Unrestricted funding – critical for organisational stability – was 44% less for organisations led by people of colour.

Multi-year grants were substantially less common for organisations led by people of colour.

These disparities reflect foundation decision-makers' (overwhelmingly white) comfort with white-led organisations and implicit bias associating white leadership with professionalism and effectiveness. Foundations perpetuate racial hierarchy through funding allocation rather than challenging it.

THE DEPENDENCY TRAP: WHEN PUBLIC GOODS REQUIRE PRIVATE WEALTH

When public services and social programmes become dependent on philanthropic funding, democratic governance is compromised. Dependency shifts accountability from citizens to donors and reduces pressure for adequate public investment.

EDUCATION DEPENDENCY

Public schools increasingly rely on foundation grants for programming, professional development, technology and facilities improvements. In many districts, foundation funding supplements inadequate public appropriations, creating dependency. Schools dependent on Gates, Walton or local foundation funding must align programmes with donor priorities rather than solely serving democratically determined educational goals.

This dependency enables philanthropic policy capture. When the Walton Family Foundation provides substantial charter school funding to a district, district officials face pressure to expand charters regardless of community preferences or evidence of charter effectiveness (Reckhow & Snyder, 2014). Financial dependency constrains democratic autonomy.

HEALTH SYSTEMS VULNERABILITY

In low-income countries, health systems' dependence on foundation funding creates acute vulnerabilities. When the Gates Foundation funds 40–60% of malaria control budgets in several African countries, those governments cannot pursue alternative approaches or resist foundation priorities without risking funding loss (Storeng, 2014). This shifts governance from national governments accountable to citizens towards a foundation accountable to donors.

COVID-19 illustrated these dependencies: countries reliant on Gates-funded vaccine infrastructure experienced supply chain disruptions when foundation priorities shifted. Democratic governments must maintain sufficient public capacity to serve citizen needs independent of philanthropic whims.

CROWDING OUT PUBLIC INVESTMENT

Philanthropic spending can reduce political pressure for adequate public investment. When billionaires fund parks, libraries, schools or social services, this diminishes electoral pressure on governments to provide these public goods through taxation and democratic appropriation. Research by economist Rob Reich (2018) demonstrates that philanthropic substitution for public goods often results in overall lower service levels and less equitable distribution than democratic public provision would produce.

Moreover, philanthropic funding is unstable: donors can withdraw support when priorities change, leaving communities without services they have come to depend on. Democratic public funding, while imperfect, provides more stable support accountable to constituents.

SOLUTION REQUIRES PUBLIC CAPACITY

Addressing dependency traps requires rebuilding public capacity through adequate taxation of concentrated wealth and democratic investment in public services. Foundations should supplement, not substitute for, democratically determined public provision. This means progressive taxation providing governments with resources to meet basic needs, reserving philanthropy for innovation, experimentation and supplementary enhancement rather than core service delivery.

7

THE RACIAL AND CLASS DIMENSIONS OF WEALTH GOVERNANCE

The preceding analysis of wealth concentration and democratic governance has largely treated wealth as if it accumulates neutrally, without systematic patterns of racial and class stratification. This chapter corrects that omission by examining how wealth accumulation, inheritance and philanthropic deployment are deeply racialised and classed processes. Understanding these dimensions is essential for designing democratic wealth governance that addresses rather than perpetuates structural inequality.

THE RACIALISATION OF WEALTH ACCUMULATION

Wealth in the United States and globally is not distributed randomly but follows clear racial patterns reflecting centuries of exploitation, exclusion and discrimination. These patterns are not historical artefacts but ongoing structural features requiring explicit attention in wealth governance.

CONTEMPORARY WEALTH GAPS

By 2023, median white family wealth in the United States was $285,000 compared to $61,000 for Latino families and just $27,000 for Black families (Federal Reserve, 2024). This means the typical white family holds 10.6 times the wealth of the typical Black family and 4.7 times that of the typical Latino family. At the top of the distribution, whites comprise 89% of the wealthiest

1%, while Black Americans – 13% of the population – represent less than 2% of top wealth holders (Survey of Consumer Finances, 2024).

These gaps are not primarily explained by income differences, education or individual behaviour. Black families at every income level, education level and occupation hold substantially less wealth than comparable white families (Hamilton & Darity, 2017). A Black household headed by someone with a college degree has less median wealth than a white household headed by someone without a high school diploma (Gittleman & Wolff, 2004). This demonstrates that wealth gaps reflect structural factors beyond individual merit or effort.

Globally, wealth disparities track colonial histories. Former colonising powers (Britain, France, Belgium, the Netherlands) and their settler colonies (the United States, Canada, Australia) hold vastly disproportionate shares of global wealth relative to formerly colonised regions in Africa, Asia, Latin America and the Caribbean. The extraction of resources, labour and wealth during colonialism created foundations for contemporary concentration in the Global North (Hickel, 2017).

These colonial wealth extraction patterns persist in contemporary global inequality. In Brazil, where slavery was abolished only in 1888 – the last Western nation to do so – Afro-Brazilians comprise 56% of the population but hold less than 25% of national wealth. White Brazilians earn on average 70% more than Black Brazilians with equivalent education, and racial wealth gaps in São Paulo rival those in US cities (Instituto Brasileiro de Geografia e Estatística, 2022). South Africa's apartheid system (1948–1994) created extreme racialised wealth concentration: by 2022, white South Africans – 7% of the population – still controlled approximately 70% of the country's land and corporate wealth, while Black South Africans held less than 10% (South African Reserve Bank, 2023). In the United Kingdom, Black Caribbean and Black African households hold median wealth of £34,000 and £24,000 respectively, compared to £314,000 for white British households (Office for National Statistics, 2022). These patterns reflect slavery, colonialism, apartheid and ongoing structural discrimination, creating racialised wealth hierarchies that wealth governance frameworks must explicitly address rather than treat as peripheral concerns.

HISTORICAL FOUNDATIONS: FROM SLAVERY TO REDLINING

Understanding contemporary racial wealth gaps requires historical analysis of how wealth accumulation was systematically racialised through law, policy and violence.

Slavery as Wealth Accumulation

American slavery (1619–1865) represented the largest forced wealth transfer in human history. Enslaved people's labour – producing cotton, tobacco, rice and sugar – generated immense fortunes for slaveholding families and financing for industrial development. By 1860, enslaved people represented $3 billion in capital value – more than all US manufacturing and railroad investment combined (Baptist, 2014). This wealth, accumulated through brutal extraction, was never compensated or redistributed after emancipation.

Many contemporary fortunes trace to slavery wealth. The Lehman Brothers investment bank was founded with profits from slavery-era cotton trading. Brown University, Georgetown University and numerous other elite institutions were built partly with slavery profits. Insurance companies like Aetna and New York Life profited from insuring enslaved people as property. Railroad and textile fortunes depended on slavery-produced cotton (Beckert, 2014).

Crucially, this wealth was transmitted intergenerationally through inheritance. White families that accumulated wealth through slavery passed it to descendants, who invested in businesses, real estate and education that generated more wealth across generations. Meanwhile, formerly enslaved people began their freedom with nothing, facing systematic exclusion from wealth-building opportunities.

Post-Emancipation Exclusion

After slavery's end, systematic policies prevented Black wealth accumulation:

Failed Land Redistribution: Following the Civil War, '40 acres and a mule' promised redistributing confiscated Confederate land to formerly enslaved families – a policy that would have created Black landownership and agricultural wealth. However, President Andrew Johnson reversed this policy in 1865, returning land to former Confederate owners and leaving freed people landless (Foner, 1988).

Convict Leasing: Southern states criminalised Black behaviour through 'Black Codes' and then leased convicted Black men to plantations, mines and construction projects under conditions approximating slavery. This system extracted wealth from Black communities while enriching white landowners and corporations through the early 20th century (Blackmon, 2008).

Jim Crow Segregation: Legal segregation confined Black Americans to lower-wage occupations, inferior schools and limited business opportunities. Exclusion from skilled trades, professions and management prevented income and wealth accumulation. Segregation persisted legally until 1964 and informally much longer.

Violent Dispossession: White mob violence destroyed Black wealth accumulation repeatedly. The 1921 Tulsa Race Massacre destroyed Greenwood, a prosperous Black neighbourhood ('Black Wall Street'), killing hundreds and eliminating $50–100 million in Black-owned property (in current dollars). Similar massacres occurred in Rosewood, Florida (1923); Wilmington, North Carolina (1898); and dozens of other communities, destroying Black businesses and property (Ellsworth, 1982).

20TH-CENTURY EXCLUSION: NEW DEAL AND GI BILL

Even ostensibly universal 20th-century wealth-building policies systematically excluded Black Americans:

Social Security Exclusions: The 1935 Social Security Act excluded agricultural and domestic workers – occupations where 65% of Black workers were employed – denying Black families access to old-age insurance and wealth accumulation that white families enjoyed (Lieberman, 1998).

Federal Housing Administration Redlining: Beginning in 1934, the Federal Home Administration (FHA) explicitly refused to insure mortgages in predominantly Black neighbourhoods – 'redlining' – preventing Black families from accessing homeownership, the primary wealth-building mechanism for American families. FHA underwriting manuals instructed appraisers to downgrade neighbourhoods with Black residents, systematically channelling capital to white suburbs while disinvesting from Black communities (Rothstein, 2017).

This policy created the enormous wealth gap we observe today. Between 1934 and 1968, 98% of FHA loans went to white families. White homeownership rates climbed from 44% in 1940 to 64% by 1970, while Black homeownership stagnated around 40% (Oliver & Shapiro, 2006). Home values in white neighbourhoods appreciated dramatically, while redlined Black neighbourhoods deteriorated from a lack of investment. Families that purchased homes with FHA assistance accumulated hundreds of thousands of dollars in home equity; excluded Black families accumulated nothing.

GI Bill Discrimination: The 1944 GI Bill provided college tuition, job training and low-interest mortgages to World War II veterans – transforming millions of working-class white families into the middle class. However, administration was delegated to states and localities, enabling systematic discrimination. Southern states denied Black veterans benefits; banks refused mortgages to Black GI Bill holders; universities excluded Black applicants. Of 67,000 mortgages insured in Mississippi and New York in 1947, fewer than 100 went to Black veterans (Katznelson, 2005).

These policies operated for decades, creating wealth accumulation opportunities for white families while systematically excluding Black families during the most significant wealth-building period in American history. The consequences compound across generations.

Contemporary Mechanisms of Racial Wealth Extraction

While explicit racial discrimination in wealth accumulation is now illegal, contemporary mechanisms continue extracting wealth from communities of colour.

Predatory Lending

Black and Latino families are disproportionately targeted for predatory mortgages, payday loans and high-cost financial products that extract rather than build wealth. During the 2000s housing bubble, Black and Latino borrowers with credit scores qualifying for prime mortgages were routinely steered to subprime loans with higher interest rates and fees (Engel & McCoy, 2011). When the housing market collapsed, Black and Latino families lost disproportionate wealth – over $194 billion in collective losses for Black households alone (Bocian et al., 2010).

Criminal Justice Extraction

The criminal justice system functions as wealth extraction from communities of colour through fines, fees, bail, asset forfeiture and incarceration costs. Black Americans are incarcerated at 5 times the rate of white Americans and Latino Americans at 1.3 times (Sentencing Project, 2022). Incarceration destroys wealth through lost wages, employment barriers upon release and collateral consequences (housing, education, professional licencing restrictions). Research shows that each year of incarceration reduces lifetime earnings by 40%, with effects concentrated in Black and Latino communities (Western, 2018).

Municipal court systems in many jurisdictions operate as revenue generators, imposing fines and fees disproportionately on Black and Latino residents for minor offences. Ferguson, Missouri – site of Michael Brown's 2014 killing – derived 23% of city revenues from court fines and fees, predominantly extracted from Black residents (Department of Justice, 2015). This pattern appears nationwide, transferring wealth from low-income communities of colour to municipal governments.

Discriminatory Employment and Wages

Labour market discrimination continues limiting wealth accumulation opportunities for people of colour. Research using randomised audit studies consistently finds that identical resumes with white-sounding names receive 50% more callbacks than those with Black-sounding names (Bertrand & Mullainathan, 2004; Quillian et al., 2017). Black college graduates face unemployment rates approximating those of white high school dropouts (Wilson & Rodgers, 2016). Wage gaps persist even controlling for education, experience and occupation, with Black workers earning 73 cents and Latino workers 83 cents for every dollar earned by comparable white workers (Economic Policy Institute, 2023).

Targeted Tax Enforcement

Recent research by Stanford economists finds that Black taxpayers face audit rates 2.9–4.7 times higher than non-Black taxpayers, even accounting for income and Earned Income Tax Credit claiming (Elzayn et al., 2024). This discriminatory enforcement extracts resources through penalties and legal costs while allowing wealthy white taxpayers – who engage in far more costly tax evasion – to avoid scrutiny.

INHERITANCE AND THE PERPETUATION OF RACIAL HIERARCHY

Intergenerational wealth transmission – inheritance, gifts, family loans – is the primary mechanism perpetuating racial wealth inequality. Wealth is far more heritable than income, and racial gaps in inherited wealth vastly exceed income gaps (Killewald et al., 2017).

INHERITANCE AS COMPOUNDING ADVANTAGE

Research by economists Darrick Hamilton and William Darity Jr. (2010) demonstrates that inheritance and inter vivos transfers (gifts) explain more of the Black–white wealth gap than any other factor, including income, education and savings behaviour. The median white family receives approximately $125,000 in lifetime inheritances and gifts; the median Black family receives less than $10,000 (Hamilton et al., 2015).

These transfers enable white families to purchase homes (down payments), finance education debt-free, start businesses and weather emergencies without depleting savings – opportunities systematically unavailable to Black families. Children of wealthy parents receive not just financial transfers but also social capital: professional networks, elite educational access, internships and cultural knowledge facilitating wealth accumulation (Pfeffer & Killewald, 2018).

Because historical exclusion prevented Black wealth accumulation, there is less wealth to inherit. A Black college graduate whose parents were excluded from homeownership and professional careers by Jim Crow has nothing to inherit, while a comparable white graduate whose parents benefited from FHA mortgages and GI Bill benefits inherits substantial wealth. This compounds across generations: inherited wealth generates investment returns that get re-inherited, creating exponential divergence.

THE RACIAL WEALTH TRANSFER IN THE COMING DECADES

Baby Boomers will transfer an estimated $68 trillion to heirs over the next 25 years – the largest intergenerational wealth transfer in history (Cerulli Associates, 2023). However, this transfer will be deeply racialised: 90% of inherited wealth will go to white families, reproducing and likely widening racial wealth gaps (Shapiro et al., 2013).

Without policy intervention, inheritance will perpetuate white wealth dominance indefinitely. Legal scholar Palma Strand (2010) argues that inheritance law – treating intergenerational wealth transfer as a private family matter beyond public concern – is a primary mechanism sustaining racial stratification. She proposes that inheritance law should explicitly consider racial equity impacts, potentially through differential taxation or wealth transfer limits that prevent dynastic perpetuation of racialised advantage.

REPARATIONS AS WEALTH GOVERNANCE

Recognition of racialised wealth accumulation has generated international reparations movements demanding accountability for historical extraction. The Caribbean Community (CARICOM) formally demanded reparations from European nations for slavery and colonialism, establishing a Reparations Commission in 2013. In 2021, the University of Glasgow committed £20 million to a reparative justice programme acknowledging its historical ties to Caribbean slavery. The Netherlands government issued a formal apology for slavery in 2023 and established a €200 million fund for awareness and educational programmes. These initiatives, while modest relative to historical harms, recognise that contemporary wealth concentrations rest on racialised extraction requiring reparative responses. Democratic wealth stewardship must integrate such reparative frameworks, acknowledging that concentrated wealth often traces to unjust accumulation.

PHILANTHROPIC PERPETUATION OF RACIAL HIERARCHY

Foundation funding patterns systematically perpetuate racial hierarchy rather than challenge it, despite philanthropic rhetoric about equity and justice.

Underfunding Organisations Led by People of Colour

As noted in Chapter 6, organisations led by people of colour receive 76 cents for every dollar that white-led organisations receive when serving similar populations (Bridgespan Group, 2020). This disparity reflects foundation decision-makers' implicit biases and social networks: foundation staff and trustees are overwhelmingly white (84% of foundation staff; 92% of trustees), drawing on predominantly white professional networks when identifying grantees (Council on Foundations, 2023).

The National Committee for Responsive Philanthropy (2020) found that even foundations with explicit racial equity commitments underinvest in organisations led by people of colour:

Only 7% of foundation funding goes to organisations explicitly focused on communities of colour despite those communities comprising 40% of the US population.

Organisations led by people of colour receive smaller grants, shorter grant terms and more restricted funding than their white-led counterparts.

Foundation initiatives addressing racial inequality are often designed and led by white staff, with people of colour in advisory rather than decision-making roles.

Elite Beneficiaries Over Working-Class Communities

Foundation funding disproportionately benefits elite institutions serving affluent populations. The largest recipients of foundation grants are elite universities (Harvard, Stanford and MIT), museums and arts organisations serving wealthy patrons and medical research institutions. Meanwhile, grassroots organisations serving low-income communities of colour – providing direct services, organising for justice and building community power – receive minimal foundation support.

Research by the National Committee for Responsive Philanthropy (NCRP) (2019) found that foundations give:

$2.50 to elite universities for every $1 to community-based organisations.

$4 to arts and culture institutions serving affluent audiences for every $1 to community development.

$6 to medical research benefiting diseases affecting affluent populations for every $1 to primary care access for underserved communities.

This allocation pattern reflects foundation trustees' social positions and cultural preferences rather than community needs or equity priorities.

Perpetuating 'White Saviour' Narratives

Philanthropy often operates through 'white saviour' frameworks where wealthy (predominantly white) donors provide resources to 'help' communities of colour, centring donor agency and expertise while marginalising community voice and leadership. This dynamic replicates colonial relationships, with communities of colour positioned as passive recipients of elite generosity rather than agents determining their own futures (Cole, 2020).

MacKenzie Scott's giving – distributing over $14 billion to 1,600 organisations since 2019 – illustrates both possibility and limitation. Scott has prioritised organisations led by people of colour, unrestricted funding and trust-based approaches without burdensome reporting. This represents a significant improvement over traditional philanthropy (Scott, 2024). However, Scott's unilateral decision-making – determining which organisations receive funding without participatory processes involving affected communities – still centres donor control. A more fully democratic approach would include participatory mechanisms where communities exercise authority over resource allocation.

Class Politics and Democratic Wealth Governance

Beyond racial dimensions, wealth concentration fundamentally reflects class stratification – the division of society into working class, middle class and capitalist class with vastly divergent economic interests and political power.

Class Analysis of Wealth Concentration

Political scientist Jeffrey Winters (2011) distinguishes between oligarchy (rule by the wealthy) and democracy (rule by the people), arguing that extreme wealth concentration inevitably produces oligarchic tendencies as wealthy individuals deploy resources to defend their material interests. Winters demonstrates that across different political systems – democracies, autocracies, mixed regimes – the ultra-wealthy constitute a distinct political class with shared interests in wealth defence: preserving property rights, minimising taxation and preventing redistribution.

This class analysis reveals that conflicts over wealth governance are not technical disputes about optimal tax rates or foundation effectiveness but fundamental struggles over power: Will economic resources be governed democratically by working-class majorities, or will they remain under elite control? Framing wealth governance as a class struggle clarifies stakes and alliances.

Working-Class Interests in Wealth Redistribution

The working class – those dependent on wages or salaries for livelihood, constituting approximately 63% of US households (Economic Policy Institute, 2023) – has clear material interests in wealth redistribution. Wealth taxes, progressive inheritance taxation and democratically controlled public investment would finance programmes directly benefiting working-class families: healthcare, education, childcare, housing, infrastructure and public services.

However, mobilising working-class political power to achieve redistribution faces structural obstacles:

Campaign Finance Plutocracy: As documented in Chapter 1, wealthy donors dominate political contributions, systematically advancing candidates opposing redistribution. Working-class candidates face enormous fundraising disadvantages, limiting electoral pathways for redistributive politics.

Media Ownership: Wealthy individuals' ownership of media enables framing political debates in terms favouring elite interests – emphasising 'economic growth', 'innovation' and 'entrepreneurship' over redistribution, equity and democratic control.

Organisational Decline: Labour unions, historically the primary institutional vehicle for working-class political power, have declined dramatically. US union membership fell from 34% of workers in 1954 to 10% by 2023 (Bureau of Labor Statistics, 2024). This organisational collapse weakened working-class political capacity.

Cross-Class Divisions: Elite manipulation of racial, ethnic and cultural divisions has historically prevented working-class solidarity. Wealthy interests benefit when white working-class voters identify with race rather than class, supporting policies serving wealthy interests while opposing redistribution that would benefit working-class people across races (Roediger, 2007; Anderson, 2016).

BUILDING CROSS-RACIAL WORKING-CLASS SOLIDARITY

Effective democratic wealth governance requires building working-class political movements that transcend racial divisions. This requires the following:

Universal Programmes With Targeted Implementation: Social programmes that are universal in eligibility but targeted in implementation to address disparities – such as Social Security (universal) with particular outreach to ensure Black and Latino enrolment – can build cross-racial working-class coalitions while addressing racial inequality (Brown et al., 2003).

Explicit Racial Justice Framing: Rather than avoiding racial inequality to maintain white working-class support, research by Ian Haney López (2014) and Anat Shenker-Osorio (2019) shows that explicit anti-racism messaging that links racial justice to shared economic interests can build multiracial working-class solidarity. Messages emphasising that 'wealthy elites use racism to divide working people' prove more effective than either colour-blind economic appeals or race-only messaging.

Labour Movement Revitalisation: Rebuilding working-class organisational power requires labour movement renewal, including sectoral bargaining, card check union recognition, strike protection and public sector union strengthening. Research demonstrates that union membership correlates strongly with both economic equality and multiracial political solidarity (Rosenfeld, 2014).

Community-Labour Alliances: Coalitions linking labour unions with community organisations representing communities of colour – such as the Fight for $15, Black Lives Matter and immigrant rights movements – can build institutional capacity for working-class political power (Milkman, 2014).

INTEGRATING RACIAL AND CLASS JUSTICE INTO WEALTH STEWARDSHIP

Democratic wealth governance must explicitly address both racial and class dimensions. This requires the following:

Reparative Redistribution

Wealth redistribution should be explicitly reparative, acknowledging that current concentration reflects historical theft and ongoing extraction. This implies the following:

Reparations for Slavery and Jim Crow: Direct payments to descendants of enslaved people, funded through wealth taxation on fortunes with slavery origins.

Targeted Wealth-Building Programmes: Baby bonds, down payment assistance and business capital prioritised for Black, Latino and Indigenous families to counteract historical exclusion.

Community-Controlled Investment: Wealth taxes funding democratically controlled community investment in neighbourhoods subjected to redlining, disinvestment and extraction.

Representative Participatory Mechanisms

Citizen oversight panels governing foundations and participatory budgeting processes must be genuinely representative of affected populations, particularly communities of colour and working-class people. This requires the following:

Stratified Random Selection: Sortition processes ensuring proportional representation by race, class, geography and other relevant dimensions.

Compensation Enabling Participation: Payment sufficient to enable working-class participation without income loss.

Capacity-Building Support: Training, facilitation and resources enabling meaningful participation by communities historically excluded from governance.

Funding Justice-Oriented Organisations

Foundations should face requirements to fund organisations led by people of colour, working-class communities and grassroots movements at levels proportional to population and need. This means:

Mandatory Minimums: Foundations must allocate at least 40% of funding to organisations led by people of colour (proportional to U.S. demographics) and 50% to organisations serving low-income communities.

Trust-Based, Unrestricted Funding: Multi-year, unrestricted grants that trust community leadership rather than impose donor-determined restrictions.

Power-Building Support: Funding for organising, advocacy and movement-building, not just service delivery.

ANTI-SUBORDINATION PRINCIPLE IN WEALTH GOVERNANCE

Legal scholar Owen Fiss (1976) proposed an 'anti-subordination principle' for constitutional equality: the goal is not merely treating people identically but dismantling systems of social hierarchy. Applied to wealth governance, this principle requires that any wealth accumulation, inheritance or philanthropic deployment that perpetuates racial or class subordination face heightened scrutiny and potential prohibition.

Concretely, this means:

Inheritance Limits Preventing Racial Hierarchy Reproduction: Stronger inheritance taxation with exemptions for transfers reducing racial wealth gaps.

Foundation Programmes Assessed for Anti-subordination: Programmes must demonstrate that they reduce rather than perpetuate racial and class stratification.

Corporate Governance Promoting Equity: Worker representation, community benefit requirements and stakeholder governance requirements that empower subordinated groups.

Key Insight: Wealth Governance Without Racial and Class Justice Is Incomplete

The framework developed in Chapters 1–6 risks remaining abstract and inadequate if it fails to address the racial and class dimensions of wealth accumulation and deployment. Wealth is not colour-blind or class-neutral; it has been accumulated through racial exploitation and class extraction, and it continues to be deployed in ways reproducing those hierarchies.

Democratic wealth governance must be explicitly committed to reparative redistribution, representative participation of subordinated communities and structural transformation of racial and class hierarchies. Only then can wealth stewardship serve genuinely democratic and egalitarian purposes rather than merely restructuring elite control.

The following chapters on policy mechanisms (Part IV) integrate these racial and class justice imperatives into concrete actions.

Part IV

SOLUTIONS

8

PRE-DISTRIBUTION: SHAPING ACCUMULATION

The Democratic Wealth Stewardship Framework operates through two complementary strategies: pre-distribution (shaping how wealth accumulates in the first instance) and post-distribution (governing how accumulated wealth is deployed). This chapter addresses pre-distribution mechanisms that prevent extreme concentration before it occurs, reducing the need for corrective redistribution afterwards.

Pre-distribution recognises that market outcomes reflect institutional rules – property rights, corporate governance, labour law, tax policy, competition regulation – that are politically determined, not natural. By reforming these rules, democratic societies can shape wealth accumulation to serve broader prosperity rather than extreme concentration.

PROGRESSIVE WEALTH TAXATION: DESIGN AND JUSTIFICATION

Wealth taxes – annual levies on net worth – directly address concentration by reducing the stock of accumulated wealth rather than merely taxing income flows. While controversial, wealth taxation has strong justifications and feasible implementation pathways.

NORMATIVE JUSTIFICATIONS

Stewardship Principle: As established in Chapter 3, extreme wealth reflects social production and creates power over others' lives. Wealth taxation embodies the principle that such resources are held in stewardship with obligations to serve public purposes.

Democratic Equality: Political equality requires constraining wealth concentration that enables policy capture, information control and political domination. Wealth taxation prevents accumulations that threaten democratic institutions.

Intergenerational Justice: Wealth taxation generates revenues for public investment and debt reduction, serving future generations' interests rather than perpetuating elite dynastic control.

Economic Efficiency: Wealth taxation encourages productive deployment rather than passive accumulation. Idle wealth parked in financial instruments or luxury consumption generates minimal social benefit; taxation incentivises productive investment or transfer to more dynamic actors.

DESIGN FEATURES

Economists Emmanuel Saez and Gabriel Zucman (2019) propose a progressive wealth tax structure for the United States:

High Exemption Threshold: Tax applies only to wealth exceeding $50 million, affecting fewer than 75,000 households (0.05% of population).

Progressive Rates: 2% annual tax on wealth between $50 and $250 million; 3% on wealth between $250 million and $1 billion; 5% on wealth exceeding $1 billion.

Comprehensive Base: Includes all assets – real estate, financial assets, business equity, art, jewellery – minus liabilities.

Valuation Rules: Market prices for traded assets; formula-based valuation for businesses; professional appraisals for art/collectibles.

This structure would generate approximately $350–400 billion annually while concentrating burdens on the ultra-wealthy who can most afford it (Saez & Zucman, 2019). Revenue could fund universal childcare, public higher education, infrastructure investment, climate action and deficit reduction.

INTERNATIONAL EXPERIENCE

Several European countries have implemented wealth taxes with varying success. Switzerland maintains cantonal wealth taxes, generating approximately 1% of tax revenues (OECD, 2024). Spain reintroduced a wealth tax in 2022 after an earlier suspension. Norway taxes net wealth exceeding NOK 1.7 million (approximately $165,000) at 1.1%, generating revenues supporting social programmes (Norwegian Tax Administration, 2024).

France's experience illustrates both possibilities and pitfalls. France implemented a wealth tax (ISF) from 1982 to 2017, but wealthy taxpayers exploited loopholes, and some relocated to avoid the tax. In 2017, France replaced the comprehensive wealth tax with a real estate-only version (IFI), reducing revenues substantially. Critics argue that France's failure resulted from design flaws – too many exemptions, low thresholds hitting middle-class families, insufficient international coordination – rather than inherent infeasibility (Landais et al., 2020).

Latin American nations have experimented with wealth taxation amid extreme concentration. Argentina implemented a one-time 'millionaire's tax' (Aporte Solidario y Extraordinario) in 2020, levying 2–3.5% on wealth exceeding 200 million pesos (approximately $2.3 million), raising $2.4 billion to fund pandemic response, medical equipment and small business support. Colombia adopted a progressive wealth tax in 2022 targeting fortunes above $1 million, with rates reaching 1% for assets exceeding $5 million, generating revenue for education and poverty reduction. Chile's 2022 constitutional debate prominently featured wealth taxation proposals, though the constitution was narrowly rejected. These experiences demonstrate that wealth taxation is politically viable in democracies facing extreme inequality, countering claims that such measures are 'impossible' or 'utopian'. They provide implementation lessons on administrative capacity, compliance mechanisms and coalition-building strategies for wealth governance reforms.

IMPLEMENTATION CHALLENGES AND SOLUTIONS

Wealth tax critics raise several objections, each addressable through careful design:

VALUATION DIFFICULTIES

Objection: Many assets lack clear market values (private businesses, art, intellectual property), making wealth calculation difficult.

Response: Valuation methods exist and are routinely used for estate taxes, property taxes and financial reporting. Private businesses can be valued using formula approaches based on revenues, earnings and comparable public companies. Taxpayers who claim low valuations can be required to sell assets at declared values to government entities, ensuring honest reporting. Professional appraisals can assess art and collectibles. Errors will occur, but they need not prevent overall fairness.

CAPITAL FLIGHT

Objection: Wealthy individuals will relocate to tax havens, eroding the tax base.

Response: Exit taxes on unrealised capital gains prevent tax-free emigration. The United States already imposes exit taxes on individuals renouncing citizenship with a net worth exceeding $2 million (IRC Section 877A). These could be strengthened to capture full unrealised appreciation at the time of exit. Additionally, international coordination – discussed below – reduces opportunities for tax avoidance through relocation.

LIQUIDITY CONSTRAINTS

Objection: Wealth-rich but income-poor individuals (e.g., farmers with valuable land) may lack cash to pay wealth taxes.

Response: Payment deferral options allow spreading payments over time or deferring until asset sale. Estate tax law already includes such provisions. Additionally, high exemption thresholds ($50 million) ensure that liquidity constraints affect only the ultra-wealthy, who can access credit markets or sell portions of assets if necessary.

ADMINISTRATIVE COSTS

Objection: Wealth tax administration requires significant IRS resources and enforcement capacity.

Response: While administrative costs exceed income tax costs, research suggests they remain manageable – approximately 2–3% of revenues raised (Saez & Zucman, 2019). Moreover, wealth tax administration investments improve overall tax enforcement by creating comprehensive wealth reporting infrastructure, reducing evasion across tax types.

TAXATION AND RACIAL WEALTH JUSTICE

Wealth taxation must explicitly address racial wealth gaps. This requires designing taxation and spending to reduce racial stratification:

Higher Rates on Inherited Wealth

Because inherited wealth perpetuates racial hierarchy (as documented in Chapter 7), inherited fortunes should face higher taxation than entrepreneurial wealth. Economist Darrick Hamilton proposes differential wealth tax rates: 1% on self-made wealth and 3% on inherited wealth, recognising that inherited fortunes carry weaker justifications and perpetuate unearned advantage (Hamilton & Darity, 2017).

Revenue Uses Targeting Racial Wealth Gaps

Wealth tax revenues should prioritise programmes reducing racial inequality:

Baby Bonds: Senator Cory Booker's proposed American Opportunity Accounts would provide children from low-wealth families with savings accounts funded from birth, accumulating to $46,000 by age 18 for the lowest-income families. Research by Hamilton and Darity (2010) estimates that this would reduce the Black-white wealth gap by 15% within one generation.

Down Payment Assistance: Targeted programmes helping Black and Latino families overcome homeownership barriers created by historical redlining

HBCU Investment: Substantial federal investment in Historically Black Colleges and Universities, addressing chronic underfunding relative to predominantly white institutions

Community-Controlled Development: Grants to community land trusts and cooperatives in communities of colour, enabling democratic wealth building

Reparations Integration

Some economists propose integrating wealth taxation with reparations for slavery and Jim Crow. The Commission to Study and Develop Reparation Proposals for African Americans, established in California in 2020, calculated that eligible Black Californians were owed approximately $569 billion in compensation for various harms (California Reparations Task Force, 2023). A federal programme would require trillions of dollars – substantial wealth taxation could provide funding while simultaneously addressing concentration.

INHERITANCE TAX REFORM: CHALLENGING DYNASTIC WEALTH

Current estate and inheritance taxation is weak, enabling dynastic wealth transmission across generations. Reform should substantially strengthen these taxes.

Current Law Weaknesses

The US estate tax applies only to estates exceeding $13.6 million per individual ($27.2 million per couple) in 2024, with a 40% rate above that threshold (IRS, 2024). However, aggressive tax planning enables many ultra-wealthy families to avoid most estate taxation through:

Grantor Retained Annuity Trusts (GRATs): Allow transferring asset appreciation tax-free to heirs.

Charitable Lead Trusts: Reduce taxable estate values by committing future income to charity while preserving principal for heirs.

Valuation Discounts: Claim that closely held business interests are worth less than proportional equity values, reducing taxable amounts.

Dynasty Trusts: Establish perpetual trusts in states without rule against perpetuities, avoiding estate tax across multiple generations.

These techniques enable families like the Waltons (Walmart fortune) to transfer tens of billions to heirs while paying minimal estate tax relative to transferred amounts (Collins & Hoxie, 2017).

REFORM PROPOSALS

Lower Exemption, Higher Progressive Rates

Senator Bernie Sanders's 'For the 99.5% Act' proposes:

Exemption Threshold: $3.5 million per individual ($7 million per couple).

Progressive Rates: 45% on estates $3.5–10 million; 50% on $10–50 million; 55% on $50 million–1 billion; 65% on estates exceeding $1 billion.

This structure would affect only the wealthiest 0.5% of estates while generating approximately $430 billion over 10 years (Sanders, 2021).

Close Loopholes

Prohibit valuation discounts for family businesses and trusts.

Restrict GRAT effectiveness by requiring minimum terms and taxing ultra-low or negative interest rate benefits.

Limit dynasty trusts by enforcing rule against perpetuities nationally.

Include grantor trust assets in taxable estates.

Shift to Inheritance Tax Model

Rather than taxing estates (at death), tax inheritances (received by heirs). This approach, common in Europe, taxes each beneficiary's lifetime total inheritances and gifts above a threshold. Under this model, receiving $10 million triggers a tax on the recipient, incentivising wealth distribution to multiple beneficiaries rather than concentration in a single heir. Legal scholar Lily Batchelder proposes a progressive inheritance tax with rates from 15 to 55% on lifetime total inheritances and gifts exceeding $2.5 million per recipient (Batchelder, 2020).

Mark-to-Market Taxation of Capital Gains

Currently, capital gains go untaxed until assets are sold, and gains held until death escape taxation entirely through 'step-up in basis' rules. This enables wealthy families to accumulate untaxed appreciation across lifetimes. Reform should tax unrealised capital gains at death (or periodically during life for the ultra-wealthy), closing this massive loophole. President Biden's 2024 budget proposal included taxing unrealised gains at death for estates exceeding $7 million (White House, 2024).

ANTITRUST ENFORCEMENT: PREVENTING MARKET POWER FROM BECOMING POLITICAL POWER

Economic concentration enables political dominance: dominant firms can threaten relocation, withhold investment or fund opposition to unfavourable policies. Vigorous antitrust enforcement prevents economic power from reaching levels that enable political capture.

Historical Foundations

Early US antitrust law recognized political dimensions. Senator John Sherman, author of the 1890 Sherman Act, argued that trusts were 'kingly prerogatives, inconsistent with our form of government' (Sherman Antitrust Act, 1890). Justice Louis Brandeis warned that concentrated economic power threatened democracy: 'We can have democracy in this country, or we can have great wealth concentrated in the hands of a few, but we can't have both' (Brandeis, 1941).

However, since the 1970s, antitrust enforcement narrowed to 'consumer welfare' measured primarily through prices. Under this approach, monopolies are permissible if they don't raise prices – ignoring political power, innovation suppression, labour monopsony and supplier exploitation. This narrow focus enabled unprecedented concentration: Amazon dominates e-commerce, Google controls search, Meta dominates social media and a handful of firms control each major industry sector.

Neo-Brandeis Antitrust

A revitalised antitrust approach incorporates political power considerations:

Structural Presumptions Against Concentration

Mergers creating firms with market share exceeding 30% should face strong presumptions against approval. Dominant platforms (search engines, social networks and app stores) should be treated as essential facilities requiring access for competitors. Companies operating platforms that compete with platform users should face structural separation requirements preventing self-preferencing.

Labour Monopsony Focus

Antitrust should address not just consumer harm but labour monopsony – employer market power suppressing wages. Research demonstrates that labour market concentration is pervasive and significantly reduces wages (Azar et al., 2020). Mergers reducing labour market competition should face scrutiny comparable to product market mergers.

Political Influence as Antitrust Factor

Merger reviews should explicitly consider political influence. When proposed mergers would create entities with substantial political lobbying capacity, campaign contribution capability or regulatory capture potential, this should weigh against approval independent of economic efficiency considerations.

Breakups of Dominant Platforms

Dominant digital platforms – Amazon, Google, Meta – should face breakup requirements separating platform operation from platform participation. For example, Amazon should not both operate a marketplace and sell competing products on that marketplace. Google should not both operate search and prioritise its own services in results. This structural separation prevents self-dealing while preserving platform benefits (Khan, 2017).

Labour Law Reform: Ensuring Workers Share in Productivity Gains

Wealth concentration reflects not just taxation and market structure but also labour's declining power relative to capital. Between 1979 and 2020, US productivity increased 62% while median worker compensation increased only 17% – the gap represents wealth transferred from labour to capital (Economic Policy Institute, 2021). Labour law reform can reverse this shift.

UNION REVITALISATION

Card Check and First Contract Arbitration

The proposed Protecting the Right to Organise (PRO) Act would enable union recognition through card-check (majority sign union cards) rather than requiring elections where employers can intimidate workers. It would also mandate binding arbitration for first contracts when negotiations stall, preventing employer delay tactics that undermine new unions (PRO Act, H. R. 842, 2023).

Sectoral Bargaining

Rather than enterprise-by-enterprise unionisation, sectoral bargaining – common in Europe – enables negotiating industry-wide standards. When unions represent entire sectors, employers cannot undercut unionised competitors by exploiting non-union workers, and workers gain bargaining power from scale. Several states have begun experimenting with sectoral approaches in healthcare, domestic work and gig economy sectors (Andrias & Rogers, 2018).

Strike Protection

Current law permits employers to permanently replace striking workers, gutting strike effectiveness. Reform should prohibit permanent replacement, ensuring strikes remain viable worker tools. Additionally, secondary strikes and boycotts – illegal under Taft-Hartley Act restrictions – should be relegalised, enabling solidarity across workplaces.

Gig Worker Classification

Workers classified as independent contractors – including many gig economy workers – lack union rights, minimum wage protections and benefits.

Reforming independent contractor tests (adopting stricter ABC tests) would extend labour protections to millions of workers currently excluded.

Worker Board Representation

As discussed in Chapters 3 and 7, worker representation on corporate boards – standard in Germany and widespread across Northern Europe – democratises corporate governance. Senator Warren's Accountable Capitalism Act would require 40% of board seats for worker-elected directors at large corporations (Warren, 2018).

Research demonstrates that codetermination does not harm firm performance while improving working conditions, reducing inequality and increasing employment stability (Jäger et al., 2021). Workers with governance voice can resist wealth extraction through stock buybacks, executive compensation and financialisation, instead directing surpluses towards wages, benefits and productive investment.

Asian models offer additional pathways for democratising corporate governance and limiting wealth concentration. South Korea's chaebol reform movement has pushed for enhanced transparency, independent board representation and limits on family control of conglomerates like Samsung and Hyundai, where founding families control assets exceeding $300 billion through complex ownership structures. Japan's postwar keiretsu system, while not fully democratic, distributed corporate ownership across networks of firms and employees rather than concentrating it in individual hands, contributing to Japan's relatively egalitarian wealth distribution through the 1980s. India's 2013 Companies Act mandates that profitable firms spend 2% of profits on CSR activities, creating accountability for wealth deployment, though implementation remains contested. These diverse approaches demonstrate multiple institutional pathways towards democratic governance of concentrated corporate wealth.

FINANCIAL REGULATION: CONSTRAINING RENT-SEEKING AND SPECULATION

Much wealth accumulation occurs through financial sector rent-seeking – extracting returns through market power, information asymmetries and regulatory arbitrage rather than productive contribution. Financial regulation can constrain such extraction.

PROPOSALS

Financial Transaction Tax

A small tax on financial transactions (0.1% on stock trades, 0.01% on derivatives) would reduce high-frequency trading, algorithmic speculation and short-term financial churning while generating substantial revenue. Senator Sanders and Representative Barbara Lee proposed such a tax, estimating $2.4 trillion in revenue over 10 years (Sanders & Lee, 2021). This tax would fall predominantly on financial sector actors rather than ordinary investors.

Carried Interest Loophole Closure

Private equity and hedge fund managers currently pay capital gains rates (20%) on 'carried interest' compensation rather than ordinary income rates (37%), a loophole saving them billions annually. Closing this loophole – treating compensation as income – would generate approximately $180 billion over 10 years while improving tax fairness (Joint Committee on Taxation, 2023).

Stock Buyback Restrictions

Stock buybacks – corporations repurchasing their own shares – transfer value to shareholders (disproportionately executives with stock options) without productive investment. The Inflation Reduction Act of 2022 imposed a 1% excise tax on buybacks; this should be increased to 4–8% to more effectively discourage buybacks while encouraging productive investment (Lazonick, 2014).

Increased Capital Requirements

Higher bank capital requirements reduce systemic risk while constraining financial sector extraction. After 2008 reforms, large banks face capital requirements of 7–13% of risk-weighted assets, but research suggests requirements should exceed 15% to adequately protect against crises (Admati & Hellwig, 2013).

INTERNATIONAL TAX COOPERATION: PREVENTING RACE-TO-THE-BOTTOM

Tax competition – countries lowering rates to attract mobile capital – systematically undermines progressive taxation. International coordination can prevent this race to the bottom.

OECD Minimum Tax Agreement

In 2021, 136 countries agreed to a global minimum corporate tax of 15% through the OECD/G20 Inclusive Framework (OECD, 2021). While implementation faces challenges and the rate is insufficient (economists suggest 25% would be appropriate), the agreement demonstrates feasibility of international tax coordination.

Wealth Tax Coordination

Similar coordination could extend to wealth taxation. If major economies (US, EU, UK, Japan) implemented compatible wealth taxes simultaneously, opportunities for tax avoidance through relocation would diminish dramatically. A coordinated wealth tax would include:

Harmonised Definitions: Comparable asset inclusion and valuation rules across jurisdictions.

Information Sharing: Automatic exchange of wealth information among tax authorities, as currently occurs for income through the Common Reporting Standard.

Exit Tax Reciprocity: Agreements recognising each jurisdiction's exit taxes, preventing tax-free wealth movement.

BENEFICIAL OWNERSHIP TRANSPARENCY

As discussed in Chapter 3's fifth principle, beneficial ownership registries revealing ultimate asset owners are essential for tax enforcement. International coordination requiring all jurisdictions to maintain and share beneficial ownership information would dramatically reduce evasion through shell companies and offshore vehicles.

9

POST-DISTRIBUTION: GOVERNING DEPLOYMENT

While pre-distribution shapes how wealth accumulates, post-distribution governance addresses how accumulated wealth is deployed – particularly through foundations, philanthropic vehicles and corporate structures. This chapter elaborates on democratic accountability mechanisms ensuring that concentrated resources serve public purposes.

MANDATORY CITIZEN OVERSIGHT PANELS FOR MAJOR FOUNDATIONS

As established in Chapter 3's second principle, foundations controlling significant resources should face citizen oversight with binding authority. This section specifies implementation details.

COVERAGE AND STRUCTURE

Threshold Triggering Requirement

Foundations with assets exceeding $1 billion or annual distributions exceeding $50 million must establish citizen oversight panels. This threshold captures approximately 120 foundations in the United States – those with outsized social impact (Foundation Center, 2024).

Panel Composition

Panels should include 15–25 members selected through stratified random sortition – lottery selection from affected populations, ensuring demographic representativeness:

Geographic representation: Members from all regions where the foundation operates significantly.

Racial and ethnic representation: Proportional to affected populations, with minimum representation for communities of colour.

Economic representation: Stratified selection ensuring the inclusion of low-income, working-class, middle-class and affluent members proportional to affected populations.

Expertise diversity: A mix of community members, nonprofit practitioners, academics and others with varied perspectives.

Selection processes mirror jury duty: randomly selected individuals receive invitations, with compensation and support enabling their participation.

International precedents demonstrate diverse foundation governance approaches. Germany's foundation law (Stiftungsrecht) requires foundations to serve the public good, with government oversight ensuring alignment between stated purposes and activities. German authorities audit operations, review strategic plans and intervene when foundations deviate from public benefit missions. The UK Charity Commission exercises similar oversight, investigating complaints and publishing performance assessments. India's Companies Act 2013 mandates 2% of profits for CSR activities with board oversight committees. South Africa's nonprofit law requires community consultation in strategic planning. These models offer lessons: government oversight can supplement citizen panels, mandatory public benefit requirements create accountability baselines, and graduated obligations ensure proportional governance intensity.

Terms and Compensation

Members serve 3-year terms, with one-third rotating annually to ensure continuity while preventing capture. Members receive compensation at professional rates ($75–100/hour for meetings, plus expenses), enabling working-class participation. Foundations provide staff support, technical assistance and training to enable informed panel functioning.

BINDING AUTHORITY

Panels exercise binding authority over:

Strategic priorities: Approve or reject overall foundation strategies, including focus areas, geographic scope and theory of change.

Major grants: Review and approve grants exceeding thresholds ($5 million for $1 billion foundations; scaled proportionally for larger foundations).

Policy positions: Approve foundation advocacy positions and lobbying activities.

Leadership evaluation: Assess foundation chief executive officer (CEO) and senior leadership, with authority to recommend dismissal for cause.

Investment policies: Approve endowment investment strategies, ensuring mission alignment.

Day-to-day operational decisions remain under staff control, but strategic direction requires panel approval.

OPERATIONAL DETAILS

Panels meet quarterly for 2–3 day sessions (compensated). Foundation staff prepare briefing materials, present proposals and respond to questions. Panels may request additional information, commission independent analysis and consult external experts. Decisions are made through deliberative processes followed by voting, with supermajority requirements (60–67%) for major strategic changes.

Panels publish meeting minutes, decision rationales and dissenting opinions, ensuring transparency. Foundation staff must implement panel decisions or appeal to judicial review (discussed below), ensuring binding authority.

ENHANCED DISCLOSURE REQUIREMENTS: BEYOND IRS FORM 990

Participatory grantmaking models internationally demonstrate the feasibility of democratic resource allocation. Mexico's Community Foundation Network (Red de Fundaciones) has developed participatory processes where community assemblies in marginalised neighbourhoods exercise binding authority over foundation grants addressing local priorities. Over 50 Mexican community foundations now use participatory approaches, allocating approximately $20 million annually through democratic decision-making. The Philippines' Assisi Development Foundation implements participatory grantmaking where farmer cooperatives and indigenous communities control resource allocation for rural development, achieving higher project success rates than traditional top-down grantmaking (Foundation Center Asia, 2023). Belgium's King Baudouin Foundation has piloted participatory approaches in several programmes, enabling affected communities to shape strategic priorities and evaluate outcomes. Taiwan's civil society foundations are increasingly incorporating participatory elements, with community representatives serving on grant review committees and shaping funding strategies. These international practices demonstrate that participatory grantmaking operates effectively across diverse cultural, economic and political contexts, challenging claims that democratic resource allocation is uniquely suited to specific national contexts.

Current foundation disclosure is inadequate for democratic accountability. Enhanced requirements should include the below:

Comprehensive Grant Disclosure

All grants exceeding $10,000 disclosed with the following:

- Recipient organisation name, mission and leadership demographics
- Grant amount, term and purpose
- Whether funding is restricted or unrestricted
- Evaluation criteria and expected outcomes
- Relationship between the foundation and recipient (prior grants, personal connections, etc.)

This information should be published in searchable databases within 30 days of grant awards, enabling real-time public scrutiny.

Complete Investment Portfolio Disclosure

Quarterly disclosure of endowment holdings include:

- Equity holdings (company name, number of shares, market value)
- Fixed income investments (bond issuers, amounts)
- Alternative investments (private equity, hedge funds, real estate)
- Detailed disclosure of any fossil fuel, private prison, weapons or other controversial holdings

This transparency enables assessing whether investments align with stated missions and public values.

Detailed Evaluation and Impact Reporting

Annual publication of:

- Evaluation methodologies for all major initiatives
- Evaluation findings, including failures and negative results
- Longitudinal impact assessments for multi-year initiatives
- Independent evaluator reports (not just foundation-commissioned assessments)
- Lessons learnt and course corrections based on evidence
- This reporting creates accountability for effectiveness, not just spending levels.

Political Influence Disclosure

Real-time disclosure of:

- All lobbying activities (issues, government officials contacted, positions advocated)
- All campaign contributions by the foundation, officers and board members
- All funding to organisations engaged in political activity

All foundation participation in policy coalitions or advocacy networks

This transparency makes political influence visible and contestable.

Demographic and Compensation Disclosure

Annual disclosure of:

Board and staff demographics (race, ethnicity, gender, class background)

Compensation for all employees and contractors exceeding $100,000

Relationships between board members and funded organisations

Foundation expenditures on trustee benefits, conferences, travel and overhead.

This information enables assessing whether foundations operate as public trusts or elite benefit vehicles.

COMMUNITY ADVISORY STRUCTURES: FROM CONSULTATION TO AUTHORITY

Beyond foundation-level citizen oversight panels, community advisory structures provide ongoing local input for foundations with place-based initiatives.

Implementation

When foundations undertake major place-based investments (exceeding $10 million in a defined community), they must establish community advisory councils with:

Democratic Selection: Council members are elected by community residents or selected through random sortition from affected neighbourhoods, ensuring genuine community representation rather than nonprofit professional dominance.

Binding Authority Over Local Implementation:

Councils approve:

- Specific programme designs for the community
- Selection of local implementing organisations
- Evaluation criteria and success metrics
- Modifications to programming based on community feedback
- Foundation staff design options, but councils exercise authority over final choices.

Community Benefit Requirements

Councils negotiate binding community benefit agreements specifying:

- Local hiring percentages
- Living wage requirements
- Community ownership or equity stakes in initiatives
- Environmental and displacement protections.

These agreements prevent foundations from imposing initiatives that generate unintended harms (gentrification, displacement, cultural disruption).

PARTICIPATORY GRANTMAKING: DEMOCRATISING RESOURCE ALLOCATION

As discussed in Chapters 3 and 6, participatory grantmaking extends democratic participation directly to resource allocation decisions.

Scaling Participatory Approaches

Currently, participatory grantmaking constitutes less than 2% of foundation giving (Participatory Grantmaking Community, 2024). Scaling requires the following:

Regulatory Requirements: Foundations exceeding size thresholds (e.g. $1 billion assets) should be required to allocate a minimum percentage (e.g. 25%) of annual distributions through participatory processes where affected community members exercise binding allocation authority.

Standardised Models: Develop standardised participatory grantmaking frameworks to enable replication

Open call processes: Publicly announce funding availability with clear eligibility criteria

Community review panels: Randomly selected or elected community members review applications.

Deliberative sessions: Facilitated discussions where panellists assess proposals against community-determined criteria

Binding community votes: Panellists vote on allocations, with staff implementing decisions.

Infrastructure Support: Establish technical assistance organisations supporting foundations in implementing participatory approaches, reducing barriers to adoption.

Evidence of Effectiveness

Research on participatory budgeting – analogous to participatory grantmaking – demonstrates positive outcomes. They are as follows:

Improved targeting: Community members identify needs and effective organisations that external experts overlook (Baiocchi, 2005).

Enhanced legitimacy: Participatory allocation enjoys greater community support than top-down decisions (Wampler et al., 2019).

Civic capacity building: Participation develops civic skills, political efficacy and democratic engagement among participants (Gastil et al., 2010).

Accountability improvements: Community allocators hold funded organisations accountable more effectively than distant foundation staff (Sintomer et al., 2013).

These findings suggest that participatory grantmaking can improve both democratic legitimacy and programmatic effectiveness.

Public Benefit Corporation Requirements

Corporations controlling significant wealth should face public benefit requirements ensuring stakeholder consideration beyond shareholder profit.

Benefit Corporation Model

Thirty-seven US states recognise "benefit corporations" – entities chartered to pursue both profit and public benefit (Benefit Corporation, 2024). However, benefit corporation status is voluntary, and most corporations retain traditional shareholder primacy governance.

Democratic wealth governance should require benefit corporation status for:

Corporations with market capitalisation exceeding $10 billion

Closely held corporations with revenues exceeding $5 billion

Corporations receiving substantial public benefits (tax breaks, subsidies, regulatory privileges).

Benefit corporations must ensure the following:

Stakeholder Consideration: Explicitly consider impacts on workers, communities, environment and long-term sustainability in decision-making, not just shareholder returns.

Public Benefit Reporting: Publish annual reports assessing performance on stakeholder dimensions using standardised metrics (B-Impact Assessment or similar frameworks).

Independent Auditing: Undergo periodic third-party assessment of public benefit performance, with results published publicly.

Stakeholder Enforcement: Enable stakeholders (workers, communities) to bring derivative suits when corporations breach public benefit obligations, creating legal accountability beyond shareholders.

Worker Representation on Corporate Boards

As elaborated in Chapters 3, 6 and 8, worker board representation democratises corporate governance.

Implementation Specifics

Senator Warren's Accountable Capitalism Act provides a model:

Coverage: Corporations with revenues exceeding $1 billion (approximately 3,000 US corporations employing over 40 million workers).

Representation Levels: Forty percent of board seats reserved for worker-elected directors, mirroring German codetermination.

Election Processes: Workers elect board representatives through secret ballot elections, with terms matching shareholder-elected director terms. Election administration by neutral third parties ensures fairness.

Full Board Authority: Worker directors exercise identical authority to shareholder directors – voting on CEO selection, compensation, strategy, mergers and all board matters. No separate "labour" and "shareholder" boards; integrated governance.

Protection from Retaliation: Workers participating in director elections or serving as directors receive legal protection from employer retaliation, with substantial penalties for violations.

ANTICIPATED EFFECTS

Research on codetermination suggests worker board representation would:

Reduce wealth extraction through excessive executive compensation and stock buybacks (Jäger et al., 2021)

Increase worker wages and benefits as surplus is directed towards labour rather than capital (Gorton & Schmid, 2004)

Stabilise employment by resisting short-term layoffs for financial engineering (Kim et al., 2018)

Improve long-term productivity by encouraging worker training and capital investment (Hagen, 2020)

Importantly, codetermination does not significantly reduce profitability or firm valuation, suggesting that worker representation redistributes surplus towards labour without destroying enterprise value.

RACIAL EQUITY MANDATES FOR FOUNDATION GOVERNANCE

Building on Chapter 7's analysis, foundations should face explicit racial equity requirements:

Representative Governance: Foundation boards and staff must reflect the demographics of the affected population within specified timeframes (e.g. 5 years). Proportional representation of people of colour on boards, in senior leadership and among programme officers ensures that decision-making incorporates diverse perspectives.

Equity Impact Assessment: All major initiatives must undergo a racial equity impact assessment before implementation:

Who benefits? Demographic analysis of intended beneficiaries

Who decides? Analysis of decision-making authority and community voice

What assumptions? Examination of implicit assumptions that may reflect white/elite perspectives

Whose knowledge? Assessment of whether community knowledge and leadership are centred

Assessments published publicly enable accountability for equity commitments.

Minimum Funding for Organisations Led by People of Colour: Foundations must allocate at least 40% of grant funding to organisations led by people of colour (proportional to U.S. demographics), with "led by" defined as people of colour comprising at least 50% of the board and senior leadership.

Funding Terms Equity: Organisations led by people of colour must receive funding on equivalent terms to white-led organisations: comparable grant sizes, multi-year commitments, unrestricted funding and trust-based relationships without disproportionate reporting burdens.

Anti-Subordination Review: All foundation programmes are assessed using the anti-subordination principle (Fiss, 1976): Do programmes dismantle or perpetuate racial hierarchy? Programmes perpetuating subordination require substantial justification or redesign.

EMERGENCY RESPONSE PROTOCOLS

As addressed in Chapter 3's fourth principle, genuine emergencies may require a rapid response exceeding normal deliberative timelines. However, emergency powers require careful structuring to prevent abuse.

DEFINING EMERGENCIES

Emergency authority applies only to specified crisis categories:

Natural disasters: Hurricanes, earthquakes, floods, wildfires and other natural disasters causing mass displacement or loss of life

Public health emergencies: Disease outbreaks, pandemics and acute health crises

Humanitarian crises: Armed conflicts, refugee emergencies, famine and mass atrocities

Economic downturns, political transitions or foundation-defined "strategic opportunities" do not qualify, preventing the expansion of emergency authority.

Contingent Authorisation

Citizen oversight panels pre-authorise emergency response protocols specifying:

Maximum expenditure amounts (e.g. 10% of annual budget) deployable without prior panel approval

Acceptable emergency intervention types (immediate relief, not long-term programming)

Reporting requirements (within 72 hours of emergency expenditure)

Retrospective review timelines (within 60 days)

This framework enables rapid response while maintaining accountability.

Retrospective Review and Accountability

Within 60 days of emergency expenditures, citizen oversight panels conduct retrospective reviews assessing the following:

Did circumstances genuinely constitute qualifying emergencies?

Were responses appropriate and effective?

Were expenditures reasonable?

Were affected communities' interests prioritised?

What lessons can inform future emergency responses?

If a review reveals that emergency authority was misused – funds deployed for non-emergency purposes, excessive expenditures, inadequate community consultation – panels can impose sanctions.

Formal Censure of Leadership

Restrictions on future emergency authority

Required repayment or redirection of misused funds

In severe cases, leadership dismissal recommendations

This accountability structure preserves rapid response capacity while preventing emergency authority abuse.

10

PARTICIPATORY INNOVATIONS

The governance mechanisms outlined in Chapters 8 and 9 depend on participatory democracy – ordinary citizens exercising meaningful authority over decisions affecting their lives. This chapter examines international experience with participatory institutions, assesses evidence on scalability and proposes specific innovations for wealth governance.

INTERNATIONAL EXPERIENCE WITH PARTICIPATORY DEMOCRACY

Participatory democratic practices have proliferated globally over the past three decades, providing evidence about effectiveness, challenges and design principles.

PARTICIPATORY BUDGETING: FROM PORTO ALEGRE TO GLOBAL PRACTICE

Participatory budgeting (PB) – citizens directly deciding public budget allocations – originated in Porto Alegre, Brazil, in 1989 and has spread to over 3,000 cities across 6 continents (Participatory Budgeting Project, 2024).

Porto Alegre Model

Porto Alegre's process, operating from 1989 to 2004 under Workers' Party administrations, enabled residents to allocate significant portions of municipal capital budgets:

Neighbourhood Assemblies: Open public meetings where residents identified priorities and elected delegates.

Thematic Assemblies: Citywide meetings addressing cross-neighbourhood issues (transportation, health, education).

Budget Council: Delegates from assemblies formed a council that reviewed technical feasibility, made final allocations and monitored implementation.

Year-Round Engagement: Continuous process rather than one-time events, with monitoring committees tracking project completion.

Research by political scientist Gianpaolo Baiocchi (2005) found that Porto Alegre's PB:

Improved Service Delivery: Infrastructure investment better targeted neighbourhood needs than prior technocratic planning.

Reduced Corruption: Public visibility and citizen monitoring reduced opportunities for graft.

Enhanced Equity: Low-income neighbourhoods received proportionally more resources than under prior systems.

Built Civic Capacity: Participants developed political knowledge, efficacy and ongoing civic engagement.

Increased Satisfaction: Citizens reported higher satisfaction with municipal government and greater sense of political influence.

Global Diffusion and Adaptation

PB has spread globally with significant adaptations:

New York City: Since 2012, NYC allocates $35–40 million annually through PB in participating City Council districts. Over 500,000 residents have participated, with particularly high engagement from communities of colour and young people (PBNYC, 2024). Evaluations show that PB improves budget equity and increases political participation among historically marginalised groups.

Paris: Since 2014, Paris allocates €500 million (now reduced but still substantial) through citywide and neighbourhood PB processes, with both resident and online voting. Over 200,000 Parisians have participated annually (Ville de Paris, 2024).

Portugal national PB: Portugal implemented national-level PB in 2017, allocating €3 million initially (expanded to €5 million) for citizen-selected national projects. Over 80,000 citizens participated in the first cycle, with high youth engagement (Portuguese Government, 2024).

Seoul, South Korea: Seoul's PB allocates significant infrastructure and programme budgets through multi-stage processes combining online and offline participation, with explicit efforts to include marginalised populations (Seoul Metropolitan Government, 2024).

Kenya's national participatory budgeting, launched in 2015, enables county-level citizen participation in allocating development funds, with over 2 million Kenyans participating in budget forums by 2023 (Kenyan National Treasury, 2024). The process combines traditional community forums (baraza) with digital platforms, achieving high rural participation rates. Indonesia's Musrenbang system implements participatory planning in over 75,000 villages, enabling citizens to identify development priorities that shape municipal and provincial budgets. While implementation quality varies, research shows that villages with active Musrenbang processes achieve better service delivery outcomes. Spain's Decidim platform, developed in Barcelona, provides open-source digital infrastructure for participatory democracy, now used in over 400 cities globally for participatory budgeting, policy development and democratic deliberation. These examples demonstrate participatory democracy's scalability across low-, middle- and high-income contexts, refuting claims that democratic governance requires high state capacity or educated populations.

International Innovations in Participatory Wealth Governance

Beyond budgeting and foundation oversight, participatory approaches increasingly govern concentrated wealth deployment. Norway's Oil Fund governance, while not fully participatory, includes parliamentary oversight, civil society consultation on ethical guidelines and public transparency requirements, demonstrating democratic accountability for sovereign wealth exceeding $1.4 trillion. Scotland's land reform initiatives require community consent for large land purchases, giving rural communities participatory authority over concentrated landownership decisions. Iceland's 2010–2013 constitutional process included crowdsourced citizen input on governing economic power after the financial crisis, though Parliament ultimately blocked implementation. Ecuador's Yasuní-ITT Initiative attempted participatory decision-making over oil extraction in biodiversity zones, demonstrating possibilities (and challenges) of democratic governance over natural resource wealth. These experiments, despite mixed success, establish precedents for participatory control over extreme wealth concentration.

THE SCALABILITY QUESTION: EVIDENCE FROM IMPLEMENTATION RESEARCH

Critics argue that participatory processes work in small communities but cannot scale to large populations, complex decisions, or substantial resources. However, empirical evidence challenges this scepticism.

Evidence for Scalability

Large-Scale Implementation

PB has operated successfully in cities exceeding 1 million residents (Paris, New York, Chengdu) and has been implemented at provincial and national levels (Portugal, South Korea, Kenya). While processes adapt at scale – often using delegate systems, online platforms and hybrid formats – core participatory elements persist.

Research by political scientists Yves Sintomer et al. (2013), analysing over 1,000 PB cases globally, found no evidence that population size inherently undermines participatory effectiveness. Larger jurisdictions require different organisational approaches (more decentralised assemblies, greater digital integration), but participation quality and impact remain comparable.

Complex Technical Decisions

Citizen assemblies – randomly selected groups deliberating on complex policy issues – have addressed highly technical matters successfully. Examples include the following:

Ireland's Citizens' Assembly on Abortion (2016–2017): 99 randomly selected citizens deliberated on Ireland's constitutional abortion ban, hearing from medical experts, ethicists, lawyers and stakeholders. The assembly recommended liberalisation; subsequent referendum legalised abortion based substantially on assembly recommendations (Farrell et al., 2019).

France's Citizens' Convention on Climate (2019–2020): 150 randomly selected citizens deliberated for 9 months on climate policy, hearing from scientific experts and economists. The convention produced 149 policy recommendations, many technically sophisticated, addressing transportation, housing, agriculture and consumption (Convention Citoyenne pour le Climat, 2020).

UK's Climate Assembly (2020): 108 randomly selected citizens deliberated on achieving net-zero emissions by 2050, producing detailed policy recommendations across all economic sectors (Climate Assembly UK, 2020).

These assemblies demonstrate that ordinary citizens, provided with information, expert input, time for deliberation and skilled facilitation, can engage meaningfully with technical complexity.

ADDRESSING PARTICIPATION BIAS

Early PB initiatives often suffered from participation skewed towards educated, middle-class, politically engaged residents. However, careful design can overcome this bias:

Stratified Random Selection: Randomly selecting participants with quotas ensuring demographic representativeness (used in citizen assemblies) guarantees inclusion of marginalised groups.

Proactive Outreach and Support: Targeted recruitment, childcare provision, translation services, accessible venues and compensation enable working-class participation.

Online-Offline Hybrid Models: Combining in-person assemblies with digital participation expands access for those unable to attend meetings.

Research by Patricia García-Espín and colleagues (2024) on citizen assemblies found that when processes include compensation, childcare, transportation support and stratified selection, working-class participation reaches proportional levels. Without such support, middle-class over-representation persists.

REMAINING CHALLENGES

Scalability remains challenging in several respects:

Resource Intensity

Genuine participatory processes require significant investment in facilitation, information provision, logistical support and compensation. Porto Alegre's PB involved thousands of meetings annually with extensive city staff support. Citizen assemblies require months of sustained deliberation with professional facilitation and expert witnesses. These costs are manageable – typically 1–3% of budgets are being allocated participatively – but require commitment (Wampler, 2019).

Elite Resistance

Scaling participatory democracy threatens existing power holders – foundation trustees, corporate boards, political elites – who resist ceding authority. Successful scaling requires either supportive political leadership (as in Porto Alegre under Workers' Party governance) or social movement pressure forcing elite concessions.

Sustaining Participation Over Time

Initial enthusiasm for participatory processes can wane as novelty fades or if early participants feel their input is ignored. Maintaining engagement requires demonstrating that participation produces tangible results and that participant input genuinely shapes decisions.

Deliberative Quality at Scale

Ensuring high-quality deliberation – thoughtful discussion, diverse perspective consideration and reasoned justification – becomes more challenging at scale. Solutions include smaller deliberative groups (15–25 people) feeding into larger representative bodies, professional facilitation maintaining deliberative standards and structured protocols ensuring all voices are heard.

CITIZEN ASSEMBLIES FOR FOUNDATION OVERSIGHT

Applying citizen assembly models to foundation governance offers promising pathways for democratic oversight.

Selection Process

For each major foundation (assets exceeding $1 billion), randomly select 15–25 citizens from affected populations using stratified sampling:

Geographic Stratification: Representation from all regions where the foundation operates significantly.

Demographic Stratification: Proportional representation by race, class, age and gender.

Interest Stratification: Mix of nonprofit practitioners, community activists, academics and general public.

Selection Involves Multiple Stages: Initial random invitation (similar to jury duty), brief applications explaining interest and capacity and final lottery among qualified applicants ensuring stratification targets. Compensation enables working-class participation.

Deliberative Process

Assemblies meet quarterly for 2–3-day sessions over 3-year terms:

Information Provision: Foundation staff provide comprehensive briefings on strategy, grants, evaluation, finances and governance.

Expert Testimony: Independent experts (academics, practitioners, evaluators) offer analysis and respond to assembly questions.

Stakeholder Input: Funded organisations, affected communities and critical voices present perspectives.

Facilitated Deliberation: Professional facilitators structure discussion, ensuring all members participate, diverse perspectives are considered and reasoning remains focused.

Decision-Making: After deliberation, assemblies vote on strategic priorities, major grants and policy positions, with supermajority requirements (60–67%) for major changes.

Authority and Accountability

Assembly decisions are binding on foundations. Staff must implement assembly-approved strategies or appeal to judicial review for determinations that assembly decisions exceed statutory authority or violate legal requirements. This ensures assemblies exercise genuine authority while maintaining legal accountability.

Assemblies publish detailed rationales for decisions, enabling public scrutiny. Dissenting members can publish minority opinions, maintaining transparency about deliberative disagreements.

Rotation and Continuity

One-third of the assembly membership rotates annually, ensuring fresh perspectives while maintaining institutional knowledge. Exiting members mentor incoming members, facilitating transition.

Worker Cooperatives and Democratic Enterprise

Beyond foundations and corporations, democratic wealth governance extends to enterprise ownership structures. Worker cooperatives – businesses owned and governed by workers – provide models for democratic wealth creation and control.

INTERNATIONAL MODELS

Mondragon Corporation (Spain)

Mondragon, founded in 1956, is the world's largest worker cooperative federation, comprising over 80 cooperatives employing 80,000 workers across manufacturing, retail, finance, education and research (Mondragon Corporation, 2024). Key features include the following:

Democratic Governance: Each worker-member has one vote in cooperative governance, regardless of capital contribution. Workers elect management and board members.

Equitable Compensation: Pay ratios between highest- and lowest-paid workers are capped (typically 6:1, compared to 350:1 at large US corporations).

Profit-Sharing: Surplus is distributed partly to worker-members, partly to collective reserves for reinvestment and partly to community development.

Job Security Commitment: During economic downturns, cooperatives prioritise maintaining employment over maximising profit, with workers accepting temporary pay reductions when necessary.

Extensive Training: Mondragon invests heavily in worker education and skill development, maintaining a cooperative university and technical schools.

Research on Mondragon shows comparable productivity and innovation to conventional firms while achieving greater employment stability, lower inequality and stronger community ties (Arando et al., 2015).

Emilia-Romagna Cooperatives (Italy)

The Emilia-Romagna region of Italy hosts a dense network of cooperatives employing over 500,000 workers – approximately 30% of regional employment (Euricse, 2024). These cooperatives span manufacturing, agriculture, retail, social services and construction. The region's per capita GDP exceeds Italian and EU averages, demonstrating that cooperative economies can achieve prosperity (Zamagni & Zamagni, 2010).

The Evergreen Cooperatives (United States)

The Evergreen Cooperative Network in Cleveland, Ohio, demonstrates cooperative potential in low-income communities of colour. Launched in 2009, Evergreen includes worker-owned businesses in laundry services, solar installation, urban agriculture and energy efficiency retrofitting (Evergreen Cooperatives, 2024). Key features include:

Community Anchor Strategy: Cooperatives supply services to major nonprofit institutions (hospitals, universities) through long-term contracts, ensuring stable revenues.

Worker Ownership With Support: Workers become owners after probationary periods, with training and mentorship supporting success.

Community Wealth Building: Profits stay in communities rather than being extracted to distant shareholders.

Explicit Racial Justice Mission: Cooperatives prioritise hiring from low-income communities of colour, offering pathways to wealth building for historically excluded populations.

Evergreen demonstrates that cooperative models can function as economic development strategies in marginalised communities, building wealth democratically rather than depending on external investment.

Policy Support for Cooperatives

Democratic wealth governance should actively promote cooperative development:

Financing Support: Establish public cooperative development banks providing low-interest loans and technical assistance for cooperative formation and expansion, similar to Italy's Cooperative Development Fund.

Procurement Preferences: Government and nonprofit institutions should establish procurement preferences for cooperatives, providing stable revenue streams enabling cooperative growth.

Conversion Facilitation: When business owners retire, facilitate conversion to worker cooperatives rather than sales to outside buyers or closures. Italy's Marcora Law provides financing for worker buyouts, preserving businesses as cooperatives (Vieta, 2020).

Technical Assistance: Fund cooperative development centres providing legal, financial and management assistance to emerging cooperatives, reducing barriers to formation.

Education Integration: Incorporate cooperative business models into business school curricula and economic education, normalising cooperatives as viable enterprise forms.

Digital Platforms for Transparent Deliberation

Digital technologies can enhance participatory democracy by enabling broader inclusion, real-time transparency and continuous engagement while preserving deliberative quality.

Taiwan's vTaiwan Model

Taiwan's vTaiwan platform, developed by Digital Minister Audrey Tang, demonstrates digital participatory potential (Tang, 2019). The platform enables:

Open Proposal Submission: Citizens propose policy ideas that others can discuss and refine collaboratively.

Opinion Clustering: Algorithms identify areas of consensus and disagreement, surfacing shared values beneath surface disputes.

Iterative Deliberation: Multiple rounds of input allow participants to refine positions based on others' reasoning and new information.

Government Response: Policymakers respond to citizen proposals with commitments or explanations for rejections.

vTaiwan addressed Uber regulation, alcohol sales online and other contentious issues, achieving consensus on policies balancing competing interests (Tang, 2019). The platform demonstrates that digital deliberation can handle complexity while maintaining democratic legitimacy.

Decidim (Barcelona)

Barcelona's Decidim platform supports participatory budgeting, policy deliberation and collaborative proposal development (Decidim, 2024). Over 400,000 users across multiple cities have participated, proposing initiatives, debating alternatives and voting on implementations. Research shows Decidim enhances participation without degrading deliberative quality when combined with offline facilitation (Peña-López et al., 2020).

Design Principles for Digital Participation

Effective digital participatory platforms incorporate the following:

Accessibility: Multilingual interfaces, screen reader compatibility, low-bandwidth functionality and integration with offline processes, ensuring digital divides don't exclude populations.

Deliberation Support: Features encouraging reasoned exchange – requiring explanation for positions, highlighting diverse viewpoints, surfacing areas of agreement and disagreement – rather than simple polling.

Transparency: All input is visible (except where privacy requires confidentiality), enabling participants to see how their contributions relate to overall deliberation and final decisions.

Human-Algorithm Partnership: Algorithms assist by organising information, identifying patterns and facilitating matching between participants with complementary perspectives, but humans retain decision authority.

Linkage to Offline Processes: Digital participation integrated with in-person assemblies, ensuring that online discussions connect to binding decision-making and implementation.

INTEGRATION: RACE, CLASS AND SCALED PARTICIPATION

Successfully scaling participatory democracy for wealth governance requires explicit attention to racial and class dimensions. Without such attention, participation replicates existing inequalities.

Addressing Participation Gaps

Research consistently finds that without proactive design, participation skews towards white, educated, middle-class populations (García-Espín et al., 2024). Addressing these gaps requires the following:

Compensated Participation: Pay rates sufficient to offset lost wages, enabling working-class participation. Rates should reflect local living wages, not token stipends.

Logistical Support: Childcare, transportation, accessible venues, meal provision and flexible scheduling (evenings, weekends) reduce barriers for working-class participants, particularly women who disproportionately bear caregiving responsibilities.

Culturally Responsive Processes: Facilitation styles, meeting formats and decision-making processes adapted to diverse cultural norms. Western deliberative formats centred on formal presentations and Robert's Rules may alienate communities with different deliberative traditions.

Language Justice: Multilingual facilitation, interpretation services and translated materials ensuring non-English speakers participate fully.

Power Analysis Training: Explicit discussion of how race, class and other identities shape power dynamics in deliberation, with facilitation actively countering patterns where privileged voices dominate.

Centring Marginalised Voices

Beyond proportional representation, democratic wealth governance should centre marginalised communities' leadership:

Priority Consideration: When participatory processes generate competing priorities, systematically prioritise needs of most marginalised populations, recognising that privileged groups already enjoy advantages.

Veto Power Over Harmful Initiatives: Communities of colour and low-income communities should have authority to veto foundation or corporate initiatives that threaten harm (gentrification, displacement, environmental degradation, cultural appropriation), even if those initiatives claim overall benefit.

Resource Allocation Quotas: Minimum proportions of resources (e.g., 50% of foundation grants, 40% of participatory budgets) allocated to organisations led by and serving communities of colour and working-class populations.

Autonomous Organising Support: Fund community-based organisations to organise their own participatory processes, determining priorities and strategies independently, rather than only participating in processes organised by foundations or governments.

These design features ensure that participatory democracy serves redistributive and racial justice purposes rather than merely providing legitimacy for continued elite control.

11

IMPLEMENTATION STRATEGIES

The preceding chapters articulated a comprehensive framework for democratic wealth governance with specific policy mechanisms. However, analysis of institutional design alone is insufficient; implementation requires understanding political economy – how power operates, why reforms fail and what strategies enable success. This chapter examines lessons from past reform failures, coalition-building frameworks and realistic pathways for advancing democratic wealth governance.

UNDERSTANDING REFORM FAILURE: LESSONS FROM FRANCE AND THE UNITED STATES

Historical attempts at wealth redistribution provide cautionary lessons about implementation challenges.

France's Wealth Tax: Rise and Fall

France implemented a comprehensive wealth tax (Impôt de Solidarité sur la Fortune, ISF) from 1982 to 2017 and then replaced it with a real estate-only version (Impôt sur la Fortune Immobilière, IFI) in 2017 under President Emmanuel Macron.

Initial Implementation and Design Flaws

The ISF applied to net wealth exceeding €1.3 million (approximately $1.5 million) at rates from 0.5% to 1.5%. While the tax generated €5–6 billion annually at its peak, several design flaws undermined effectiveness:

Too-low threshold: Applying to upper-middle-class families, not just ultra-wealthy, generated middle-class opposition without collecting most revenue from top concentrations. Exemptions: Business assets received substantial exemptions, enabling wealthy individuals to restructure holdings to avoid taxation (Garbinti et al., 2021).

Unilateral implementation: France implemented the tax without international coordination, creating opportunities for tax avoidance through relocation.

Capital Flight Narrative

Opponents argued that the ISF drove wealthy individuals abroad, particularly to Belgium, Switzerland and the United Kingdom. Economist Camille Landais and colleagues (2020) examined this claim, finding:

Mobility was real but modest: approximately 0.5% of ISF taxpayers emigrated annually, concentrated among the ultra-wealthy with international mobility.

However, the political salience of emigration stories – high-profile individuals like actor Gérard Depardieu renouncing citizenship – created a perception of crisis.

Lost revenue from emigration was partly offset by deterring excessive wealth accumulation and generating revenue from remaining taxpayers.

Political Coalition Failure

The ISF's repeal in 2017 reflected political coalition dynamics:

Macron, a centrist former investment banker, campaigned on wealth tax repeal, framing it as necessary for economic competitiveness.

The Socialist Party, historically supporting wealth taxation, had lost credibility after failing to address unemployment during François Hollande's presidency (2012–2017).

No strong progressive coalition mobilised to defend the ISF – labour unions focused on other issues, while middle-class voters affected by the tax didn't vigorously support it.

Wealthy interests – through media ownership, think tank funding and direct lobbying – shaped debate framing around capital flight rather than inequality or revenue needs.

Lessons

France's experience suggests the following:

Design Matters: Thresholds must target ultra-wealthy, not upper-middle class. Loopholes must be closed aggressively.

International Coordination Is Crucial: Unilateral wealth taxation creates avoidance opportunities that coordinated implementation would prevent.

Political Coalitions Require Cultivation: Progressive taxation needs organised constituencies – labour, community organisations, progressive advocates – actively defending it against well-resourced opposition.

Framing Battles Matter: When opponents control debate framing (emphasising capital flight over inequality), reforms become vulnerable even when substantively sound.

US Estate Tax Erosion

The US estate tax provides another cautionary example of reform reversal through sustained political opposition.

Historical Strength

The modern estate tax, established in 1916, reached its peak during the mid-20th century with rates up to 77% on estates exceeding $10 million (inflation-adjusted). It generated significant revenue while limiting dynastic wealth transmission (Joint Committee on Taxation, 2023).

Sustained Opposition Campaign

Beginning in the 1990s, conservative organisations – heavily funded by wealthy families facing estate taxation – launched a multi-decade campaign to eliminate the 'death tax':

- Language Reframing: Renaming the estate tax as the 'death tax' suggested ordinary families were affected, obscuring that it applied only to ultra-wealthy estates.
- Coalition Building: Mobilising small business owners and farmers with claims (largely false) that estate taxes forced business sales and farm liquidations (Graetz & Shapiro, 2005).
- Political Pressure: Sustained lobbying and campaign contributions from wealthy donors opposing estate taxation, coupled with think tank studies arguing economic harm.
- Incremental Erosion: Rather than outright repeal (which faced political obstacles), opponents secured incremental erosions – higher exemptions, lower rates – that cumulatively gutted the tax.

Results

The federal estate tax exemption increased from $600,000 in 1997 to $13.6 million by 2024 (with automatic doubling for couples). Rates fell from 55% to 40%. These changes reduced estates subject to tax from 7.6% in 1997 to less than 0.1% by 2024, while revenue fell from 1.1% of federal revenues to 0.5% (Tax Policy Center, 2024).

Lessons

The estate tax erosion demonstrates the following:

- Sustained Elite Opposition Can Reverse Reforms: Even broadly popular policies (estate tax repeal polled poorly) can be eroded through elite pressure, strategic framing and incremental changes.
- Complexity Enables Stealth Erosion: Few citizens track technical changes to exemption thresholds or rate structures, enabling erosion without public awareness.

Counter-Mobilisation Requires Resources: Progressive organisations lacked resources matching the wealthy opposition, limiting the capacity to defend the estate tax.

Framing Disadvantages Accumulate: Once 'death tax' framing took hold, progressive reformers struggled to reframe the debate around inherited privilege and opportunity inequality.

Latin American experiences offer successful coalition-building lessons contrasting with French and US failures. Brazil's 1988 Constitutional Assembly included unprecedented civil society participation, with popular amendments signed by over 12 million citizens shaping constitutional provisions on wealth, property rights and social obligations. This coalition-building created durable progressive frameworks that survived subsequent political shifts. Chile's recent constitutional processes (2019–2022) demonstrated how crisis moments – social uprising driven by inequality – create political openings for wealth governance reforms, even when specific proposals face rejection. The mobilisation itself shifted political possibility boundaries. Argentina's 2020 millionaire's tax succeeded through coalition-building among labour unions, feminist movements (taxation funding gender equity programmes) and pandemic-response advocates, demonstrating how crisis contexts enable progressive taxation when coalitions link wealth governance to urgent needs. Uruguay's plebiscite tradition shows how direct democracy mechanisms enable circumventing elite legislative resistance, with citizens directly voting on progressive reforms.

ASIAN IMPLEMENTATION PATHWAYS

Asian contexts demonstrate implementation pathways beyond Western models. South Korea's chaebol reform movements achieved incremental corporate governance changes through sustained civil society pressure, shareholder activism and judicial challenges despite elite resistance. The Citizens' Coalition for Economic Justice mobilised millions supporting transparency and accountability reforms. Taiwan's Sunflower Movement in 2014 described by Rowen (2015) showed how youth-led civic mobilisation forces government responsiveness on economic governance issues, creating political space for subsequent democratic reforms. India's Right to Government of India. (2005). achieved through grassroots organising, created a transparency infrastructure applicable to foundation and corporate governance, demonstrating how transparency reforms enable subsequent accountability measures. Japan's post-war reforms, though externally imposed initially, were sustained through coalition-building among labour unions, farmers and progressive parties, offering lessons on consolidating democratic economic governance against elite opposition.

BUILDING REFORM COALITIONS: THE HOLLAND AND SCHNEIDER FRAMEWORK

Political scientists Dorothy Holland and David Schneider (2019) analyse successful social movement campaigns, identifying key elements of reform coalitions. Applied to wealth governance, their framework suggests:

Coalition Components

Moral Framing

Successful reform coalitions articulate clear moral narratives connecting policy to broadly shared values. For wealth governance, effective frames include the following:

Fairness: 'Everyone should contribute to society based on ability to pay; inherited billionaire wealth violates fairness.'

Opportunity: 'Every child deserves a fair start; extreme wealth concentration denies opportunity to ordinary families.'

Democracy: 'Democracy means one person, one vote – not one dollar, one vote. Billionaire political influence undermines democracy.'

Intergenerational Responsibility: 'We owe future generations a liveable planet and opportunity. Concentrated wealth enables short-term extraction threatening our children's futures.'

Research by cognitive linguist George Lakoff (2014) and messaging strategist Anat Shenker-Osorio (2019) demonstrates that moral framing resonates more powerfully than technocratic arguments about optimal tax rates or economic efficiency.

Multi-Constituency Alliances

Effective coalitions unite diverse constituencies with shared interests in wealth governance reform:

Labour Unions: Workers benefit from wealth taxation funding public investment, labour law reform and constraining employer power.

Racial Justice Organisations: Communities of colour benefit from reparative redistribution, participatory governance and funding for community-controlled development.

Environmental Organisations: Climate action requires massive investment financed through wealth taxation and democratically controlled resources.

Small Business Associations: Competitive markets require antitrust enforcement, preventing dominant firms from crushing small competitors.

Faith Communities: Religious traditions across denominations emphasise economic justice, wealth obligations and care for vulnerable populations.

Youth Movements: Young people facing the climate crisis, student debt and diminished opportunity have clear stakes in wealth redistribution.

Building these coalitions requires identifying shared interests while respecting each constituency's autonomy and leadership.

INSIDE–OUTSIDE STRATEGY

Effective reform combines institutional pressure (electoral politics, lobbying, litigation) with movement mobilisation (protests, strikes, civil disobedience):

Inside: Electoral campaigns for progressive candidates, legislative advocacy for specific policies, administrative rulemaking, strategic litigation.

Outside: Mass mobilisations demonstrating public support, direct action disrupting business-as-usual and strike threats credibly demonstrating movement power.

Neither strategy alone suffices. Inside-only approaches get captured by elite compromise; outside-only approaches lack mechanisms to translate pressure into policy. Combined strategies – movements mobilising to support friendly officials while applying pressure when officials waver – prove most effective (Hacker & Pierson, 2016).

NARRATIVE INFRASTRUCTURE

Sustaining reform requires 'narrative infrastructure' – media, research institutions and communication capacity amplifying reform messages:

Alternative Media: Independent journalism and content creation not dependent on wealthy ownership.

Progressive Think Tanks: Policy research organisations generating technical analysis supporting reform.

Academic Engagement: Scholars conducting rigorous research on wealth inequality, democratic governance and policy effectiveness.

Communication Capacity: Skilled communicators translating complex policy into accessible narratives reaching broad audiences.

Building this infrastructure requires investment – philanthropic support, membership dues and public funding – creating capacity to counter well-funded conservative narrative infrastructure.

CONTEMPORARY REFORM MOVEMENTS: ELIZABETH WARREN AND WEALTH TAX ADVOCACY

Senator Elizabeth Warren's 2020 presidential campaign, centred on a wealth tax proposal, demonstrates contemporary reform coalition-building in practice.

Proposal Design

Warren's Ultra-Millionaire Tax proposed:

Two percent annual tax on household wealth between $50 and $1 billion.

Three percent annual tax on wealth exceeding $1 billion (later increased to 6%).

Estimated revenue: $3.75 trillion over ten years.

Enforcement: Increased IRS funding, exit taxes, international cooperation.

The proposal, developed with economists Emmanuel Saez and Gabriel Zucman, incorporated lessons from international experience – high thresholds, progressive rates and robust enforcement (Warren, 2020).

Coalition Building

Warren's campaign built multi-constituency support:

Labour Alignment: Proposed using wealth tax revenue to fund universal childcare, public education, infrastructure and other programmes benefiting working families, securing union support.

Racial Justice Integration: Explicitly connected wealth taxation to racial wealth gaps, proposing that revenues fund baby bonds, HBCU investment and reparative programmes, gaining support from racial justice organisations.

Climate Connection: Proposed wealth tax revenue funding Green New Deal implementation, securing climate movement support.

Anti-Corruption Framing: Emphasised wealth concentration's threat to democracy, connecting taxation to political reform, resonating across the ideological spectrum.

Billionaire Contrast: Made billionaires symbols of system failure – 'billionaires shouldn't exist' – creating a stark moral contrast that energised progressive base.

Public Reception

Polling showed strong public support: 74% of registered voters supported Warren's wealth tax, including 57% of Republicans (Reuters/Ipsos, 2020). This demonstrated that wealth taxation can attract broad support when properly framed and designed.

LIMITATIONS

Warren's campaign faced obstacles. They are as follows:

Elite Opposition: Billionaires and financial sector actors vocally opposed the proposal, funding opposition research and media criticism.

Implementation Scepticism: Critics questioned administrative feasibility and effectiveness, concerns amplified by media coverage.

Democratic Party Establishment Resistance: Moderate Democrats, concerned about business community reaction, preferred incremental approaches over structural reform.

Coalition Fragmentation: While Warren built broad support, coalition members sometimes prioritised different issues (unions focused on labour law, climate groups on Green New Deal, racial justice groups on reparations), diffusing pressure behind wealth taxation specifically.

Lessons

Warren's campaign demonstrates the following:

Public Appetite for Wealth Redistribution Exists: Contrary to elite assumptions, bold redistributive proposals attract majority support when well-designed and compellingly framed.

Elite Opposition Remains Formidable: Wealthy interests deploy substantial resources – media access, funded opposition research, campaign contributions – against reforms threatening their interests.

Coalition Breadth Matters: Connecting wealth taxation to multiple constituencies' priorities builds broader support than single-issue campaigns.

Implementation Details Affect Credibility: Technical policy design matters; serious proposals with credible enforcement mechanisms attract greater support than vague populist rhetoric.

THE COALITION ARCHITECTURE OF SUSTAINABLE REFORM

Synthesising these lessons suggests that sustainable wealth governance reform requires multi-layered coalition architecture:

Electoral Coalition

Candidates committed to democratic wealth governance running for executive and legislative positions.

Campaign platforms explicitly connecting wealth governance to constituent priorities (healthcare, education, climate, racial justice).

Small-donor fundraising infrastructure reducing dependence on wealthy contributors.

Electoral mobilisation targeting progressive base while persuading moderate voters through moral framing.

Movement Infrastructure

Labour unions organising workplaces and mobilising members for political action.

Racial justice organisations centring communities of colour's leadership and priorities.

Climate justice movements connecting wealth concentration to environmental destruction.

Faith-based organising drawing on religious traditions' economic justice teachings.

Youth movements emphasising intergenerational stakes.

Coalition coordinating bodies facilitating cooperation without suppressing constituency autonomy.

Research and Policy Capacity

Progressive think tanks producing technical policy analysis.

Academic researchers conducting rigorous studies on inequality and democratic governance.

Legal organisations pursuing strategic litigation.

Policy advocates developing legislative proposals and supporting friendly lawmakers.

Communication Ecosystem

Independent media providing journalism not beholden to wealthy owners.

Digital organising platforms enabling rapid mobilisation.

Messaging strategists developing effective frames and narratives.

Cultural producers (artists, writers, filmmakers) creating content normalising wealth governance reform.

Strategic Sequencing for Political Momentum

Reform implementation should follow strategic sequencing – ordering policies to build momentum, demonstrate effectiveness and weaken opposition:

Phase One: Democracy Reforms

Begin with reforms strengthening democratic institutions, creating conditions enabling subsequent wealth governance such as the following:

Campaign finance reform reducing wealthy donor influence.

Voting rights protection and expansion increasing working-class political power.

Media ownership restrictions limiting billionaire information control.

Union protection facilitating labour movement revitalisation.

These reforms don't directly address wealth concentration but strengthen democratic capacity to pursue redistribution.

Phase Two: Revenue Generation

Implement taxation raising substantial revenue while building public confidence by:

restoring estate tax to historical levels with loophole closure;

implementing progressive wealth taxation starting with very high thresholds;

closing corporate tax loopholes and raising rates on high earners;

implementing financial transaction taxes.

Revenue enables funding popular programmes, demonstrating public investment benefits and building support for further reform.

Phase Three: Institutional Governance

With revenue flowing and democratic strength enhanced, implement governance reforms:

Citizen oversight panels for major foundations.

Enhanced disclosure and transparency requirements.

Worker board representation mandates.

Antitrust enforcement against concentrated market power.

These reforms restructure governance, embedding democratic accountability in wealth deployment.

Phase Four: Ownership Transformation

Finally, pursue deeper structural changes to ownership and control through the following:

Support for worker cooperative development.

Community wealth-building initiatives.

Public options in key sectors (banking, digital platforms, utilities).

Sectoral bargaining enabling labour power across industries.

This sequencing builds from achievable reforms (democracy protections) to more ambitious transformations (ownership restructuring), with each phase creating conditions enabling the next.

The International Dimension: Learning from the Organisation for Economic Cooperation and Development (OECD) Tax Coordination

As noted, international coordination is crucial for wealth taxation effectiveness. The 2021 OECD/G20 global minimum corporate tax agreement provides a model.

OECD Process

The OECD Inclusive Framework on Base Erosion and Profit Shifting (BEPS) brought together 136 countries to address corporate tax avoidance. After years of negotiation, countries agreed to the following:

15% global minimum corporate tax rate.

Reallocation of taxing rights, ensuring profits are taxed where economic activity occurs.

Implementation timeline with coordinated adoption.

While the 15% rate is insufficient (economists suggest 25%), the agreement demonstrates the feasibility of international tax coordination (OECD, 2021).

Wealth Tax Coordination

Similar processes could advance wealth tax coordination through the following:

Harmonised Definitions: Agreement on what assets are included, how they're valued and what constitutes taxable wealth.

Information Exchange: Automatic sharing of wealth information among tax authorities, extending the Common Reporting Standard to comprehensive wealth data.

Coordinated Implementation: Major economies agreeing to implement compatible wealth taxes simultaneously, reducing avoidance opportunities.

Exit tax Reciprocity: Agreements recognising each jurisdiction's exit taxes, preventing tax-free wealth movement.

Coordination need not be universal initially. A coalition of major economies (the United States, EU, the United Kingdom, Japan, Canada, Australia) represents sufficient market power that wealthy individuals cannot easily relocate outside the coordinated zone without sacrificing market access, residence preferences or cultural connections.

THE RACIAL JUSTICE IMPERATIVE FOR REFORM COALITIONS

Sustainable wealth governance reform requires centring racial justice, not treating it as peripheral. This means:

Leadership by People of Colour

People of colour, particularly Black and Indigenous communities bearing disproportionate harms from wealth concentration, should exercise leadership in reform coalitions. This requires the following:

Resources flowing to organisations led by people of colour.

Coalition decision-making structures ensuring people of colour have authority, not just advisory roles.

Acknowledging racial capitalism's centrality to wealth accumulation.

Reparative Framing

Wealth redistribution should be framed explicitly as reparative – addressing theft and extraction – not merely addressing inequality. This frame acknowledges historical wrongs while building multiracial working-class solidarity around shared interest in wealth democratisation.

Targeting Resources

Wealth tax revenues and participatory governance must prioritise communities of colour and working-class populations. Otherwise, reforms risk reproducing inequalities under nominally democratic structures.

Learning from Movement History

Historical social movements – Civil Rights Movement, labour organising, poor people's campaigns – provide models for multiracial coalition-building. Learning from the successes and failures of these movements can inform contemporary strategy (Theoharis, 2018).

REALISTIC ASSESSMENT: THE LONG GAME

Democratic wealth governance will not be achieved quickly or easily. Entrenched wealth concentrations and the power they enable will resist fiercely. Reform requires sustained organising across decades, not single election cycles.

Anticipated Opposition

Wealth holders will deploy every available resource to prevent reform through the following:

Campaign contributions supporting opponents and threatening reform supporters.

Media campaigns emphasising capital flight, economic harm and implementation difficulties.

Litigation challenging reforms' constitutionality and statutory authority.

International coordination obstruction leveraging relationships with foreign governments to prevent tax cooperation.

Cultural production normalising wealth concentration as natural, earned or beneficial.

Sources of Hope

Despite formidable obstacles, several factors support cautious optimism through the following:

Public Support: Majorities across democracies support wealth redistribution and constraining billionaire power when proposals are clearly articulated.

Crisis Conditions: Climate emergency, inequality's social costs and democratic threats create urgency that can overcome resistance to change.

Generational Shifts: Younger generations express greater support for structural economic reform and democratic participation than older cohorts.

Movement Capacity: Contemporary social movements – Black Lives Matter, Fight for $15, Sunrise Movement, MeToo – demonstrate renewed capacity for mobilisation.

Policy Sophistication: Progressive policy development has advanced substantially; comprehensive, technically credible proposals exist for implementation when political opportunities arise.

Democratic wealth governance is achievable but requires recognising it as a multi-generational project demanding sustained effort, strategic patience and adaptability to changing political conditions. The framework and mechanisms articulated in this book provide a roadmap; implementation depends on democratic movements building sufficient power to overcome elite resistance.

CONCLUSION: CHOOSING DEMOCRACY

This book argues that extreme wealth concentration poses an existential threat to democratic governance while simultaneously representing accumulated resources that, if properly governed, could address urgent global challenges. The central question is not whether concentrated wealth should exist – that debate oversimplifies complex realities – but rather: Who governs wealth, through what processes, accountable to whom and for what purposes?

These challenges transcend national boundaries. From Chile's constitutional debates over wealth taxation to South Korea's ongoing chaebol reform movements, from Norway's Oil Fund demonstrating democratic resource governance to India's grappling with billionaire influence in electoral politics, democracies worldwide confront similar tensions between concentrated private wealth and collective self-governance. The racial dimensions of wealth concentration, rooted in colonialism, slavery and ongoing extraction, manifest differently across contexts but share common features: persistent gaps (US Black-white wealth ratio 1:10, UK Pakistani-white 1:5, Brazil Black-white 1:3), philanthropic reproduction of these hierarchies and exclusion from wealth governance institutions.

The answer offered here is the Democratic Wealth Stewardship Framework: a comprehensive approach treating concentrated wealth as power requiring democratic authorisation, ongoing accountability and public justification. This framework rests on five interdependent principles:

Reframing property from absolute ownership to stewardship, recognising wealth's social origins and public obligations

Institutionalising meaningful democratic participation, not merely consultation, in wealth accumulation and deployment

Embedding intergenerational justice in governance through mechanisms representing future generations' interests

Managing deliberation-effectiveness tensions through institutional designs enabling both legitimacy and timely action

Ensuring authoritarian resilience through transparency, structural safeguards and comprehensive accountability

The framework's concrete proposals include wealth taxation starting at $50 million (2–5% progressive rates), mandatory citizen oversight for foundations exceeding $1 billion in assets, participatory grantmaking requirements (25% of budgets) and inheritance tax reform targeting dynastic accumulation above $10 million. These principles translate into concrete policy mechanisms operating through pre-distribution (progressive wealth taxation, inheritance reform, antitrust enforcement, labour law reform, financial regulation, international coordination) and post-distribution (citizen oversight panels, enhanced disclosure, participatory grantmaking, worker board representation, community benefit requirements, racial equity mandates).

THE RACIAL AND CLASS JUSTICE TEST

Throughout this analysis, we have emphasised that democratic wealth governance without explicit attention to racial and class dimensions remains incomplete and potentially reproduces hierarchies under nominally democratic structures. Concentrated wealth in contemporary societies reflects centuries of racial exploitation – slavery, colonialism, segregation, redlining, discriminatory enforcement – and ongoing class extraction through labour suppression, financialisation and market power.

Any framework claiming to democratise wealth governance must answer: Does this reform reduce or perpetuate racial and class stratification? Policies that fail this test – no matter how procedurally democratic – do not achieve genuine democratic governance but merely restructure elite control with participatory legitimation.

Meeting this test requires the following:

Reparative redistribution: Wealth transfers explicitly addressing historical theft and ongoing extraction from communities of colour

Representative participation: Ensuring that governance institutions reflect affected populations, particularly marginalised communities, through stratified selection, compensated participation and power-sharing commitments

Targeted resource allocation: Minimum funding requirements for organisations led by and serving communities of colour and working-class populations

Anti-subordination principle: Heightened scrutiny of any wealth accumulation or deployment perpetuating racial or class hierarchy

These elements are not peripheral additions but foundational requirements for legitimate democratic wealth governance.

CONFRONTING TRADE-OFFS HONESTLY

Democratic wealth stewardship involves real trade-offs that must be acknowledged rather than dismissed. They are as follows:

Speed Vs. Deliberation

Democratic deliberation takes time; crises demand rapid response. The framework addresses this tension through tiered deliberation (routine decisions streamlined, strategic choices receiving fuller engagement), contingent emergency powers with retrospective review and structured expert input within democratic processes. However, tension persists: some urgent problems will receive slower responses under democratic governance than under autocratic or technocratic alternatives.

The critical question is: What values are non-negotiable? This framework insists that human dignity, political equality and democratic accountability are non-negotiable, even when they impose time costs. Sacrificing democracy for speed, however urgent the crisis, may be treats people as means rather than ends, contradicting foundational moral principles. It is better to solve problems more slowly while preserving dignity than to achieve rapid 'solutions' through domination.

Efficiency Vs. Equity

Market-driven resource allocation often produces efficient outcomes in narrow economic senses but systematically generates inequitable distributions. Democratic governance prioritises equity, potentially accepting some efficiency costs. For example, participatory budgeting may allocate resources less 'efficiently' than technocratic optimisation but more equitably by incorporating community priorities that efficiency metrics ignore.

Here, the framework rejects narrow efficiency definitions that treat inequality as costless. When 'efficiency' calculations ignore distributional consequences, dignity affronts and political legitimacy erosion, they measure the wrong things. True efficiency accounts for all costs and benefits, including non-monetised values like participation, dignity and solidarity. Properly measured, democratic governance often proves more efficient than autocratic or technocratic alternatives by incorporating local knowledge, building legitimacy and preventing mistakes that narrower expertise overlooks.

Innovation Vs. Democratic Control

Rapid technological innovation in artificial intelligence, biotechnology and digital platforms creates governance lags where democratic institutions struggle to respond before technologies become entrenched. This tension is real and concerning. However, the solution is not surrendering democratic control to innovators but rather accelerating democratic institutional adaptation while establishing precautionary principles requiring democratic authorisation before deploying technologies with profound social consequences.

This means that regulatory frameworks should assume that innovations affecting millions require democratic approval rather than permissionless deployment followed by reactive regulation. It also means substantially increased public investment in the technical capacity of democratic institutions, enabling informed engagement with complexity. And it means recognising that some innovations may need to proceed more slowly or not at all if they cannot be reconciled with democratic values.

Global Scale Vs. Democratic Legitimacy

Many contemporary challenges – climate change, pandemic disease, financial stability, AI governance – are inherently global, yet democratic governance operates primarily at national and local scales. International institutions like the UN, WHO and IMF lack democratic legitimacy and enforcement capacity, while national democracies struggle to coordinate action.

This tension is perhaps the most difficult. The framework addresses it through international coordination mechanisms (tax cooperation, beneficial ownership transparency, platform regulation coordination) while acknowledging that fully democratising global governance remains an aspirational goal rather than an immediately achievable reality. Pragmatically, this means:

Strengthening democratic institutions at scales where they function (local, national, regional), building capacity for effective action;

Pursuing international coordination on specific issues (taxation, climate, financial regulation) where functional cooperation is feasible even in the absence of comprehensive global democratic governance;

Preventing undemocratic global private governance by constraining the capacity of concentrated wealth to establish parallel governance systems without accountability.

Global democracy remains incomplete, but this does not justify surrendering to undemocratic alternatives (autocratic great power coordination, technocratic expert governance or plutocratic private governance). Incremental progress towards democratic coordination is preferable to abandoning democratic principles altogether.

POLITICAL ECONOMY REALISM

This book has analysed institutional design extensively, but implementation depends fundamentally on political power. The Democratic Wealth Stewardship Framework will not be enacted through technocratic persuasion alone; it requires building political coalitions with sufficient power to overcome wealthy elites' fierce resistance.

Chapter 11 outlined coalition-building strategies, but political economy realism requires acknowledging several hard truths such as the following:

WEALTH WILL RESIST USING EVERY AVAILABLE TOOL

Concentrated wealth enables resistance through campaign contributions, lobbying, media ownership, think tank funding, litigation, international coordination obstruction and cultural production normalising inequality. Reformers must anticipate this opposition and build countervailing power through labour unions, community organisations, social movements and electoral coalitions.

REFORMS WILL BE PARTIAL, REVERSIBLE AND CONTESTED

Even successful reforms will be incomplete, will face erosion attempts and will require constant defence. The US estate tax's erosion from the 1990s through 2020s illustrates this dynamic. Sustaining reforms requires ongoing mobilisation, not just initial enactment victories.

CRISES CREATE OPENINGS

Major reforms historically occur during crises – Great Depression, World War II, civil rights movements, financial collapse – when normal political constraints loosen and change becomes possible. The 2008 financial crisis created openings that reformers inadequately exploited; future crises (climate disasters, financial instability, democratic emergencies) will create opportunities requiring preparation and rapid mobilisation.

INTERNATIONAL COORDINATION FACES FREE-RIDER PROBLEMS

Tax havens and non-cooperative jurisdictions profit from undermining coordination. Effective international action requires major economies forming coalitions with sufficient market power to impose costs on non-participants (through sanctions, market access restrictions, financial sector exclusions). This power politics is unavoidable in international tax cooperation.

REFORM IS MULTI-GENERATIONAL

Democratic wealth governance will not be achieved in a single election cycles or presidential term. It requires sustained organising over decades, building institutional capacity, developing leadership and maintaining vision through inevitable setbacks. Social Security, civil rights protections and environmental regulations required decades of organising before enactment; democratic wealth governance will similarly demand long-term commitment.

CRISIS AND OPPORTUNITY

We live in a moment of compounding crises: a climate emergency threatening civilisation's material foundations; democratic backsliding across dozens of countries; surging inequality concentrating wealth and power; disruptive technological change outpacing governance capacity; and pandemic disease revealing systemic vulnerabilities. These crises share a common feature: they are fundamentally governance crises, reflecting our collective failure to govern concentrated power democratically.

Climate change results from fossil fuel corporations' unchecked power to profit from extraction while externalising costs onto future generations. Democratic backsliding reflects the capture of information systems, electoral processes and policy-making institutions by concentrated wealth. Inequality is a result of labour's declining power relative to capital and tax policies that favour wealth over work. Technological disruption reflects private corporations' control over innovation without democratic accountability. Pandemic mismanagement reflects privatised health infrastructure and international coordination failures.

These crises create immense suffering but also political opportunity. When existing systems visibly fail – when hurricanes devastate coastlines, when democracies elect demagogues, when young people face diminished prospects despite rising productivity, when algorithms radicalise users, when pandemics expose health system inadequacies – conditions for transformative change emerge. People become willing to consider alternatives that appear unthinkable during normal times.

The Democratic Wealth Stewardship Framework offers a comprehensive alternative: not piecemeal adjustments or technocratic tweaks but fundamental restructuring of how concentrated resources are governed. It proposes treating wealth as what it actually is – accumulated social power requiring democratic accountability – rather than perpetuating fictions of absolute private ownership beyond collective concern.

Recent developments offer grounds for optimism. Argentina's 2020 millionaire tax, Brazil's participatory constitutional process, Taiwan's Sunflower Movement and Scotland's land reform demonstrate that cross-class coalitions can achieve democratic wealth governance reforms.

Climate urgency, populist energy across the political spectrum and growing recognition of inequality's democratic costs create political openings that earlier generations lacked.

THE CHOICE BEFORE US

Ultimately, the question is not technical but moral and political: What kind of society do we want?

One path leads towards plutocratic oligarchy: wealth concentration continuing unchecked, democratic institutions further eroded by money's influence, governance increasingly privatised through philanthropy and corporate power and ordinary citizens reduced to subjects of elite decision-making. This path may offer efficiency, innovation and dynamism in narrow economic senses, but it sacrifices political equality, human dignity and democratic self-governance. It treats most people as means to elite ends rather than as free and equal citizens entitled to shape collective futures.

Some argue that benevolent oligarchy – enlightened billionaires deploying wealth wisely – is tolerable or even desirable. Bill Gates saving millions of lives, Bloomberg fighting climate change and Patagonia's Chouinard protecting wilderness demonstrate potential benefits of concentrated wealth. However, even the most benevolent oligarchy remains an oligarchy: unelected, unaccountable and fundamentally undemocratic. It positions ordinary people as recipients of elite generosity rather than agents exercising self-governance. And it depends entirely on oligarchs' virtue – a dependence that democracy was created to avoid.

The alternative path leads towards democratic wealth stewardship: concentrated resources governed through participatory institutions with binding citizen authority, transparent operations enabling accountability, structural safeguards preventing anti-democratic weaponisation and explicit commitments to racial and class justice. This path treats people as free and equal, entitled to meaningful participation in decisions affecting their lives. It embeds resources in democratic relationships rather than treating them as private domains beyond collective accountability.

This democratic path involves real challenges: deliberation takes time; participation requires investment; conflicts among legitimate interests must be navigated; and some wealthy individuals will relocate or resist. But these challenges pale beside the moral imperative of treating people with dignity and the practical necessity of governance structures that can address existential threats through democratic means rather than authoritarian or plutocratic imposition.

The choice is ours to make collectively. Not through individual consumer choices or philanthropic gestures but through democratic political action: organising workplaces, building coalitions, electing committed representatives, mobilising movements and demanding fundamental reform. The framework, principles and mechanisms elaborated in this book provide a roadmap. Walking the path requires political courage, strategic patience and sustained collective effort.

Democracy is not a gift bestowed by elites but a practice of ordinary people exercising power over conditions shaping their lives. Democratic wealth governance is the extension of this practice to the domain of concentrated resources. It asserts that wealth, like political authority, ultimately belongs to the people and must be governed through processes that respect human dignity, political equality and collective self-determination.

We stand at a pivotal point in history. The decisions we make – or fail to make – about governing concentrated wealth will shape whether our children inherit a democratic, sustainable, equitable world or a dystopia of climate catastrophe, authoritarian domination and permanent hierarchy. The stakes could not be higher. The time to act is now.

The question is not whether democratic wealth stewardship is necessary – it is – but whether we possess the collective will to build it. This book argues that we must. The work of building begins with understanding, proceeds through organising and culminates in transformation. May this analysis contribute to that essential, urgent and profoundly democratic project.

ABOUT THE AUTHOR

Nancy S. Lind is a Professor Emerita of Political Science at Illinois State University, where she specialised in constitutional law, public policy and democratic governance. Her research focuses on the intersection of economic power and democratic institutions, examining how concentrated wealth shapes political processes and policy outcomes. She has published extensively on topics including executive power, separation of powers, policy analysis and the challenges facing contemporary democracies.

Her scholarly work bridges normative political theory and empirical policy analysis, seeking to identify institutional mechanisms that can preserve democratic accountability while addressing urgent public challenges. Her teaching and research have consistently emphasised the importance of citizen participation, institutional design and the structural factors that enable or constrain democratic self-governance.

This book represents the culmination of years of research on wealth concentration, democratic theory and comparative governance institutions. It synthesises insights from constitutional law, political economy and policy studies to develop a comprehensive framework for governing concentrated wealth democratically.

REFERENCES

Acemoglu, D., & Robinson, J. A. (2012). *Why nations fail: The origins of power, prosperity, and poverty.* Crown Business.

Admati, A. R., & Hellwig, M. (2013). *The bankers' new clothes: What's wrong with banking and what to do about it.* Princeton University Press.

Aliapoulios, M., Papasavva, A., Ballis, D., Zannettou, S., Blackburn, J., Stringhini, G., Sirivianos, M., & De Cristofaro, E. (2021). The gospel according to Q: Understanding the QAnon conspiracy from the perspective of information flows. In *Proceedings of the web conference 2021* (pp. 547–558). https://doi.org/10.1145/3442381.3449903

Anderson (2024). Regulation (EU) 2024/1689 of the European Parliament and of the Council of 13 June 2024 laying down harmonised rules on artificial intelligence (artificial intelligence act). *Official Journal of the European Union L, 1689.* https://eur-lex.europa.eu/eli/reg/2024/1689/oj

Anderson, E. (2016). *Private government: How employers rule our lives (and why we don't talk about it).* Princeton University Press.

Andrias, K. E., & Rogers, W. B. (2018). Rebuilding labor law for a democratic economy. *The Yale Law Journal, 127*(1), 2–70.

Arando, S., Gago, M., Kato, T., & Jones, D. C. (2015). Assessing Mondragon: Stability and managed change in the face of globalization. *Industrial and Labor Relations Review, 68*(2), 399–425. https://doi.org/10.1177/0019793914564967

Arnstein, S. R. (1969). A ladder of citizen participation. *Journal of the American Institute of Planners, 35*(4), 216–224.

Arun, T. (2019). Digital financial inclusion and the sustainable development goals. *World Development, 123*, 104623. https://doi.org/10.1016/j.worlddev.2019.104623

Azar, J., Schmalz, M. C., & Tecu, I. (2020). Anti-competitive effects of common ownership. *The Journal of Finance*, *75*(4), 1513–1565. https://doi.org/10.1111/jofi.12885

Baiocchi, G. (2005). *Militants and citizens: The politics of participatory democracy in Porto Alegre*. Stanford University Press.

Baptist, E. E. (2014). *The half has never been told: Slavery and the making of American capitalism*. Basic Books.

Barkan, J. (2018). The philanthropic complex. *Dissent*, *65*(3), 85–94.

Batchelder, L. L. (2020). Leveling the playing field between inherited income and income from work through an inheritance tax. *Tax Law Review*, *73*(1), 1–74.

Beckert, S. (2014). *Empire of cotton: A global history*. Vintage.

Been, V. (2010). Community benefit agreements: A new local government tool or another variation on the exactions theme? *University of Chicago Law Review*, *77*(1), 5–35.

Benefit Corporation. (2024). *State by state status of legislation*. https://benefitcorp.net

Bertrand, M., & Mullainathan, S. (2004). *Are Emily and Greg more employable than Lakisha and Jamal? A field experiment on labor market discrimination*. American Economic.

Bill & Melinda Gates Foundation. (2022). *Foundation endowment policy and spend-down commitment*. https://www.gatesfoundation.org

Bill & Melinda Gates Foundation. (2024). *Annual report 2024*. https://www.gatesfoundation.org

Birn, A. E. (2014). Philanthrocapitalism, past, and present: The Rockefeller Foundation, the Gates Foundation, and the setting(s) of the international health agenda. *Hypothesis*, *12*(1), e8.

Blackmon, D. A. (2008). *Slavery by another name: The re-enslavement of Black Americans from the Civil War to World War II*. Doubleday.

Bloomberg Billionaires Index. (2025). *Daily ranking of the world's richest people*. Bloomberg.

Bloomberg Philanthropies. (2024). *Climate change: Annual progress report*. https://www.bloomberg.org/environment/

Bocian, D. G., Li, W., & Ernst, K. S. (2010). *Foreclosures by race and ethnicity: The demographics of a crisis.* Center for Responsible Lending.

Brandeis, L. D. (1941). *The Brandeis guide to the modern world.* Little, Brown and Company.

Brown, M. K., Carnoy, M., Currie, E., Duster, T., Oppenheimer, D. B., Shultz, M. M., & Wellman, D. (2003). *Whitewashing race: The myth of a color-blind society.* University of California Press.

Bureau of Labor Statistics. (2024). *Union members summary.* U.S. Department of Labor.

California Reparations Task Force. (2023). *Final report.* State of California Department of Justice.

Cavanagh, S. (2014, October 21). *Gates foundation's small-schools initiative.* Education Week.

Cerulli Associates. (2023). *The Cerulli report: U.S. high-net-worth and ultra-high-net-worth markets 2023.* https://www.cerulli.com/reports/us-high-net-worth-and-ultra-high-net-worth-markets-2023

Charity Commission for England and Wales. (2024). *Annual report and accounts 2023-24.* UK Government.

Chetty, R., Friedman, J. N., Saez, E., Turner, N., & Yagan, D. (2017). Mobility report cards: The role of colleges in intergenerational mobility. *Quarterly Journal of Economics, 132*(3), 1353–1423.

Citizens United v. Federal Election Commission, 558 U.S. 310 (2010). https://supreme.justia.com/cases/federal/us/558/310/

Climate Action Tracker. (2024). *Temperatures: Addressing global warming.* https://climateactiontracker.org

Climate Assembly UK. (2020). *The path to net zero.* House of Commons.

Cohen, J. (1997). Deliberation and democratic legitimacy. In J. Bohman & W. Rehg (Eds.), *Deliberative democracy: Essays on reason and politics* (pp. 67–91). MIT Press.

Cole, T. (2020). *The white savior industrial complex.* Haymarket Books.

Collins, C., & Hoxie, J. (2017). *Billionaire bonanza: The Forbes 400 and the rest of us.* Institute for Policy Studies.

Columbia Journalism Review. (2023). *The Bezos effect: Ten years of ownership at the Washington Post.* https://www.cjr.org/

Companies House. (2024). *Register of overseas entities*. UK Government.

Congressional Budget Office. (2022). *How CBO estimated the budgetary effects of the prescription drug provisions in the inflation reduction act*. https://www.cbo.gov/

Convention on Biological Diversity. (2022). *Kunming-Montreal global biodiversity framework*. United Nations.

Costanza, R., de Groot, R., Sutton, P., van der Ploeg, S., Anderson, S. J., Kubiszewski, I., Farber, S., & Turner, R. K. (2014). Changes in the global value of ecosystem services. *Global Environmental Change*, 26, 152–158.

Council on Foundations. (2023). *Grantmaker salary and benefits report*. https://cof.org/content/2023-grantmaker-salary-and-benefits-report

Crawford, K. (2021). *Atlas of AI: Power, politics, and the planetary costs of artificial intelligence*. Yale University Press.

Credit Suisse. (2024). *Global wealth report 2024*. https://www.ubs.com/us/en/wealth-management/insights/global-wealth-report.html

Creemers, R. (2018). China's social credit system: An evolving practice of control. *SSRN Electronic Journal*. https://doi.org/10.2139/ssrn.3175792

Dasgupta, P. (2021). *The economics of biodiversity: The Dasgupta review*. HM Treasury.

Davies, N. (2014). *Hack attack: The inside story of how the truth caught up with Rupert Murdoch*. Faber & Faber.

Decidim. (2024). *Decidim: Free open-source participatory democracy for cities and organizations*. https://decidim.org

DeepMind. (2024). *AlphaFold: A solution to a 50-year-old grand challenge in biology*. Google DeepMind.

Department of Justice. (2015). *Investigation of the Ferguson police department*. U.S. Department of Justice, Civil Rights Division.

Dore, R. P. (1959). *Land reform in Japan*. Oxford University Press.

Dwyer-Lindgren, L., Bertozzi-Villa, A., Stubbs, R. W., Morozoff, C., Mackenbach, J. P., van Lenthe, F. J., Mokdad, A. H., & Murray, C. J. L. (2017). Inequalities in life expectancy among US counties, 1980 to 2014. *JAMA Internal Medicine*, *177*(7), 1003–1011.

Echoing Green, & Bridgespan Group. (2020). *Racial equity and philanthropy: Disparities in funding for leaders of color leave impact on the table.* The Bridgespan Group and Echoing Green.

Economic Policy Institute. (2021). *The productivity-pay gap.* https://www.epi.org/

Economic Policy Institute. (2023). *State of working America 2023.* https://www.epi.org/

Edelman. (2024). *2024 Edelman trust barometer: Global report.* https://www.edelman.com/trust/2024/trust-barometer

Ehrenberg, R. (1928). *Capital and finance in the age of the renaissance: A study of the Fuggers and their connections.* Jonathan Cape.

Electoral Commission. (2014). *Scottish independence referendum: Report on the voting.* UK Electoral Commission.

Ellsworth, S. (1982). *Death in a promised land: The Tulsa race riot of 1921.* Louisiana State University Press.

Elzayn, H., Smith, E., Hertz, T., Guage, C., Ramesh, A., Fisher, R., Ho, D. E., & Goldin, J. (2024). *Measuring and mitigating racial disparities in tax audits.* Stanford Institute for Economic Policy Research.

Energy Convention Citoyenne pour le Climat. (2020). *Les propositions de la Convention Citoyenne pour le Climat.* https://www.conventioncitoyennepourleclimat.fr/

Engel, K. C., & McCoy, P. A. (2011). *The subprime virus: Reckless credit, regulatory failure, and next steps.* Oxford University Press.

Esaiasson, P., Gilljam, M., & Persson, M. (2019). Responsiveness beyond policy satisfaction: Does the practice of direct democracy matter? *Comparative Political Studies, 52*(2), 163–193.

Euricse. (2024). *World cooperative monitor 2023.* European Research Institute on Cooperative and Social Enterprises.

Evaluation Office, Bill & Melinda Gates Foundation. (2022). *Evaluation of the foundation's global health portfolio.* https://www.gatesfoundation.org/about/evaluation

Evergreen Cooperatives. (2024). *Our companies.* https://www.evgoh.com

European Commission. (2022). Regulation (EU) 2022/2065 of the European Parliament and of the Council of 19 October 2022 on a single market for digital services (Digital Services Act). *Official Journal of the European Union*, *277*, 1–102. https://eurlex.europa.eu/eli/reg/2022/2065/oj

Farrell, D. M., Suiter, J., & Harris, C. (2019). The 'cognitive bonus' of assembly: How deliberation affects voting on the Irish abortion referendum. *Electoral Studies*, *57*, 176–183.

Fast, S., & Mabee, W. (2015). Place-making and trust-building: The influence of policy on host community responses to wind farms. *Energy Policy*, *81*, 27–37.

Federal Reserve. (2022). *Survey of consumer finances (SCF)*. Board of Governors of the Federal Reserve System.

Federal Reserve. (2024). *Survey of consumer finances (SCF)*. Board of Governors of the Federal Reserve System.

Fenner, F., Henderson, D. A., Arita, I., Jezek, Z., & Ladnyi, I. D. (1988). *Smallpox and its eradication*. World Health Organization.

Fink, L. (2022). *Larry Fink's 2022 letter to CEOs: The power of capitalism*. BlackRock.

Fishkin, J. S. (2018). *Democracy when the people are thinking: Revitalizing our politics through public deliberation*. Oxford University Press.

Fiss, O. M. (1976). Groups and the equal protection clause. *Philosophy & Public Affairs*, *5*(2), 107–177.

Foa, R. S., Klassen, A., Slade, M., Rand, A., & Williams, R. (2020). *The global satisfaction with democracy report 2020*. Bennett Institute for Public Policy, University of Cambridge.

Foa, R. S., & Mounk, Y. (2016). The danger of deconsolidation: The democratic disconnect. *Journal of Democracy*, *27*(3), 5–17.

Foa, R. S., & Mounk, Y. (2017). The signs of deconsolidation. *Journal of Democracy*, *28*(1), 5–15.

Foner, E. (1988). *Reconstruction: America's unfinished revolution* (pp. 1863–1877). Harper & Row.

Food and Agriculture Organization. (2020). *Global forest resources assessment 2020*. United Nations.

Forbes. (2017, September 19). *The world's billionaires list*. https://www.forbes.com/billionaires/

Forbes. (2025). *The world's real-time billionaires.* https://www.forbes.com/billionaires/

Foundation Center. (2024). *Foundation transparency: A progress report.* https://candid.org/

Foundation Center. (2025). *Key facts on U.S. foundations.* https://candid.org/

Foundation Center Asia. (2023). *Participatory philanthropy in Asia.* https://candid.org/

Foundation Directory Online. (2024). *Top funders.* Candid.

Framtidspanelet. (2025). *Citizens' panel on future generations: Annual report.* https://www.framtidspanelet.no/

Free Press. (2024). *Media consolidation: The state of the industry.* https://www.freepress.net/

Freedom House. (2024). *Freedom in the world 2024: The mounting damage of flawed elections and armed conflict.* https://freedomhouse.org/

Friedman, L., & Tankersley, J. (2022, August 7). *For Democrats, a climate bill that's both a triumph and a compromise.* The New York Times.

Garbinti, B., Goupille-Lebret, J., & Piketty, T. (2021). Accounting for wealth-inequality dynamics: Methods, estimates, and simulations for France. *Journal of the European Economic Association*, *19*(1), 620–663. https://doi.org/10.1093/jeea/jvaa025

García-Espín, P., Ganuza, E., & Vicente, M. I. (2024). *Inequality in deliberative democracy: A systematic review.* Political Studies Review.

Gastil, J., Brossard, D., & Scheufele, D. A. (2010). *The group entity: The deliberative effects of the citizens' initiative review.* University of Washington.

Gavi, the Vaccine Alliance. (2024). *Facts and figures.* https://www.gavi.org/

Gest, J., Reny, T., & Mayer, J. (2018). Roots of the radical right: Nostalgic deprivation in the United States and Britain. *Comparative Political Studies*, *51* (13), 1694–1719.

Gilens, M., & Page, B. I. (2014). Testing theories of American politics: Elites, interest groups, and average citizens. *Perspectives on Politics*, *12*(3), 564–581.

Gittleman, M., & Wolff, E. N. (2004). Racial differences in patterns of wealth accumulation. *Journal of Human Resources*, *39*(1), 193–227.

Global Polio Eradication Initiative. (2024). *Polio now*. https://polioeradication.org/

Gorton, G., & Schmid, F. A. (2004). Capital, labor, and the firm: A study of German codetermination. *Journal of the European Economic Association*, 2 (5), 863–905.

Gosseries, A. (2008). On future generations' future rights. *The Journal of Political Philosophy*, *16*(4), 446–474.

Government of India. (2005). *The right to information act, 2005 (Act No. 22 of 2005)*. Ministry of Law and Justice, Legislative Department. https://www.indiacode.nic.in/bitstream/123456789/19840/1/right_yo_information_act.pdf

Graetz, M. J., & Shapiro, I. (2005). *Death by a thousand cuts: The fight over the estate tax*. Princeton University Press.

Gross, J. (2008). Community benefits agreements: Definitions, values, and legal enforceability. *Journal of Affordable Housing & Community Development Law*, *17*(1–2), 35–58.

Guardian Media Group. (2024). *The Scott trust: Ownership and values*. https://www.google.com/search?q=https://www.theguardian.com/about/the-scott-trust

Gutmann, A., & Thompson, D. (2004). *Why deliberative democracy?* Princeton University Press.

Häberlein, M. (2012). *The Fuggers of Augsburg: Pursuing wealth and honor in Renaissance Germany*. University of Virginia Press.

Habermas, J. (1996). *Between facts and norms: Contributions to a discourse theory of law and democracy* (W. Rehg, Trans.). The MIT Press. (Original work published 1992).

Hacker, J. S., & Pierson, P. (2016). *American amnesia: How the war on government led us to forget what made America prosper*. Simon & Schuster.

Hagen, T. (2020). *Codetermination and firm performance*. German Economic Institute.

Haggerty, J. H., Haggerty, M. N., Roemer, K., & Rose, J. (2018). Planning for the local impacts of coal facility closure: Emerging strategies in the U.S. West. *Resources Policy*, *57*, 69–80.

Hallmann, C. A., Sorg, M., Jongejans, E., Siepel, H., Hofland, N., Schwan, H., Stenmans, W., Müller, A., Sumser, H., Hörren, T., Goulson, D., & de Kroon, H. (2017). More than 75 percent decline over 27 years in total flying insect biomass in protected areas. *PLoS One*, *12*(10), e0185809.

Hamilton, D., Biu, O., Famighetti, C., Green, A., Nieves, E., & Zewde, N. (2015). *Umbrellas don't make it rain: Why studying and working hard isn't enough for Black Americans*. The New School.

Hamilton, D., & Darity Jr., W. (2010). Can 'baby bonds' eliminate the racial wealth gap in putative post-racial America? *The Review of Black Political Economy*, *37*(3–4), 207–216.

Hamilton, D., & Darity Jr., W. (2017). The political economy of education, financial literacy, and the racial wealth gap. *Federal Reserve Bank of St. Louis Review*, *99*(1), 19–33.

Haney López, I. (2014). *Dog whistle politics: How coded racial appeals have reinvented racism and wrecked the middle class*. Oxford University Press.

Hern, A. (2023, July 29). *How Elon Musk broke Twitter*. The Guardian.

Heron Foundation. (2024). *Our investment approach*. https://www.heron.org/

Hickel, J. (2017). *The divide: A brief guide to global inequality and its solutions*. William Heinemann.

Holland, D. C., & Schneider, D. (2019). *Social movements and the transformation of American health care*. Oxford University Press.

InfluenceMap. (2021). *The carbon policy footprint: The 50 most influential trade associations and companies on climate lobbying*. https://influencemap.org/

International Consortium of Investigative Journalists. (2016). *The Panama Papers: Exposing the rogue offshore finance industry*. ICIJ. https://www.icij.org/investigations/panamapapers/. Accessed on April 3, 2025.

International Consortium of Investigative Journalists. (2021). *Pandora Papers: An investigation of offshore havens and hidden riches of world leaders and billionaires*. ICIJ. https://www.icij.org/investigations/pandorapapers/. Accessed on October 3, 2021.

Institute for Policy Studies. (2024). *Billionaire bonanza 2024*.

Institute on Taxation and Economic Policy. (2018). *The final 2017 federal tax bill: Policy implications*.

Instituto Brasileiro de Geografia e Estatística. (2022). *Desigualdades sociais por cor ou raça no Brasil*.

Intergovernmental Panel on Climate Change. (2023). *Climate change 2023: Synthesis report*. https://www.ipcc.ch/

Intergovernmental Science-Policy Platform on Biodiversity and Ecosystem Services. (2019). *Global assessment report on biodiversity and ecosystem services*. https://www.ipbes.net/

Internal Revenue Service. (2024). *Estate tax*. U.S. Department of the Treasury. https://www.irs.gov/businesses/small-businesses-self-employed/estate-tax

International Union for Conservation of Nature. (2024). The IUCN red list of threatened species.

Jäger, S., Schoefer, B., & Heining, J. (2021). Labor in the boardroom. *Quarterly Journal of Economics*, *136*(2), 669–725.

Jamison, D. T., Summers, L. H., Alleyne, G., Arrow, K. J., Berkley, S., Binagwaho, A., Bustreo, F., Evans, D., Feachem, R. G. A., Frenk, J., Ghosh, G., Goldie, S. J., Guo, Y., Gupta, S., Horton, R., Kruk, M. E., Mahmoud, A., Mohohlo, L. K., Ncube, M., … Yamey, G. (2013). Global health 2035: A world converging within a generation. *The Lancet*, *382*(9908), 1898–1955.

Jenkins, R., & Goetz, A. M. (2010). Accounts and accountability: Theoretical implications of the right-to-information movement in India. *Third World Quarterly*, *20*(3), 603–622.

Joint Committee on Taxation. (2023). *Estimates of federal tax expenditures for fiscal years 2023–2027*. U.S. Congress.

Jonas, H. (1984). *The imperative of responsibility: In search of an ethics for the technological age*. University of Chicago Press.

Kalla, J. L., & Broockman, D. E. (2016). Campaign contributions facilitate access to congressional officials: A randomized field experiment. *American Journal of Political Science*, *60*(3), 545–558.

Katznelson, I. (2005). *When affirmative action was white: An untold history of racial inequality in twentieth-century America*. W. W. Norton & Company.

Kenyan National Treasury. (2024). *Public participation in budget process*.

Khan, L. M. (2017). Amazon's antitrust paradox. *The Yale Law Journal*, *126* (3), 710–805.

Killewald, A., Pfeffer, F. T., & Schachner, J. N. (2017). Wealth inequality and accumulation. *Annual Review of Sociology*, *43*, 379–404.

Kim, E. H., Maug, E., & Schneider, C. (2018). Labor representation in governance as an insurance mechanism. *Review of Finance*, *22*(4), 1251–1289.

Kleinman, D. L., Delborne, J. A., & Anderson, A. A. (2017). Engaging citizens: The high cost of citizen participation in high technology. *Public Understanding of Science*, *20*(2), 221–240.

Knight, W. (2023, November 22). *Sam Altman's firing and rehiring at OpenAI*. Wired.

Knill, C., & Steinbacher, C. (2021). The trade-off between transparency and efficiency in EU decision-making. *Journal of European Public Policy*, *28*(8), 1239–1257.

Lakoff, G. (2014). *The all new don't think of an elephant!: Know your values and frame the debate*. Chelsea Green Publishing.

Landais, C., Saez, E., & Zucman, G. (2020). *A progressive European wealth tax to fund the European COVID response*. VoxEU.

Landemore, H. (2012). *Democratic reason: Politics, collective intelligence, and the rule of the many*. Princeton University Press.

Landemore, H. (2015). Inclusive constitution-making: The Icelandic experiment. *The Journal of Political Philosophy*, *23*(2), 166–191.

Lazonick, W. (2014). Profits without prosperity. *Harvard Business Review*, *92*(9), 46–55.

Levitsky, S., & Ziblatt, D. (2018). *How democracies die*. Crown.

Lieberman, R. C. (1998). *Shifting the color line: Race and the American welfare state*. Harvard University Press.

Locke, J. (1689). *Two treatises of government*. https://www.gutenberg.org/ebooks/7370

MacCulloch, D. (2003). *Reformation: A history*. Viking.

Margalit, Y., & Vega, L. (2023). *Economic inequality and the decline of political trust*. World Politics.

Marguerite Casey Foundation. (2021). *Equal voice for America's families: Lessons learned*. https://caseygrants.org/

Mayer, J. (2016). *Dark money: The hidden history of the billionaires behind the rise of the radical right*. Doubleday.

McGoey, L. (2015). *No such thing as a free gift: The Gates Foundation and the price of philanthropy*. Verso.

Mellers, B., Ungar, L., Baron, J., Ramos, J., Gurcay, B., Fincher, K., Scott, S. E., Moore, D., Atanasov, P., Swift, S. A., Murray, T., Stone, E., & Tetlock, P. E.

(2014). Psychological strategies for winning a geopolitical forecasting tournament. *Psychological Science, 25*(5), 1106–1115.

Meta. (2024). *Meta reports fourth quarter and full year 2023 results.* https://about.meta.com/

Milkman, R. (2014). Immigrant workers, precarious work, and the US labor movement. *Globalizations, 11*(3), 361–372.

Mondragon Corporation. (2024). *About us.* https://www.mondragon-corporation.com

Mueller, R. S. (2019). *Report on the investigation into Russian interference in the 2016 presidential election.* U.S. Department of Justice.

Muro, M., Liu, S., Whiton, J., & Kulkarni, S. (2019). *The geography of AI.* Brookings Institution.

Murphy, L., & Nagel, T. (2002). *The myth of ownership: Taxes and justice.* Oxford University Press.

Nathan Cummings Foundation. (2020). *Investment policy statement.* https://nathancummings.org/

National Committee for Responsive Philanthropy. (2019). *Pennies for progress: A decade of philanthropic investment in social justice.* https://www.ncrp.org/

National Committee for Responsive Philanthropy. (2020). *Power moves: Your essential philanthropy assessment guide for equity and justice.* https://www.ncrp.org/

National Institutes of Health. (2024). *Budget and spending.* U.S. Department of Health and Human Services. https://www.nih.gov/

National Philanthropic Trust. (2024). *2024 DAF report.* https://www.nptrust.org/

Nobel Foundation. (2024). *Nobel prize facts.* https://www.nobelprize.org/

Norges Bank Investment Management. (2024). *The fund.* https://www.nbim.no/

Norris, P., & Inglehart, R. (2019). *Cultural backlash: Trump, Brexit, and authoritarian populism.* Cambridge University Press.

Norway Government Pension Fund. (2024). *Responsible investment 2023.* https://www.nbim.no/

Norwegian Tax Administration. (2024). *Wealth tax.* https://www.skatteetaten.no/en/

Nussbaum, M. C. (2011). *Creating capabilities: The human development approach*. Belknap Press.

OECD. (2021). *International community strikes a ground-breaking tax deal to address the challenges arising from the digitalisation of the economy*. Organisation for Economic Co-operation and Development.

OECD. (2022). *Building trust to reinforce democracy: Key findings from the 2021 OECD survey on drivers of trust in public institutions*. Organisation for Economic Co-operation and Development.

OECD. (2024). *Revenue statistics 2023*. Organisation for Economic Co-operation and Development. https://www.oecd.org/

Office for National Statistics. (2022). *Wealth in Great Britain: Total wealth*. UK Government.

Office of the United Nations High Commissioner for Human Rights. (2022). *Assessment of human rights concerns in the Xinjiang Uyghur Autonomous Region*. People's Republic of China.

Oliver, M. L., & Shapiro, T. M. (2006). *Black wealth/white wealth: A new perspective on racial inequality*. Routledge.

OpenAI. (2023). *GPT-4 technical report*. https://openai.com/

OpenSecrets. (2021). *Revolving door*. https://www.opensecrets.org/

OpenSecrets. (2024). *Lobbying data summary*. https://www.opensecrets.org/

OpenSecrets. (2025). *2024 election fundraising*. https://www.opensecrets.org/

Oposa v. Factoran G. R. No. 101083 (Supreme Court of the Philippines 1993). https://lawphil.net/judjuris/juri1993/jul1993/gr_101083_1993.html

Oxfam. (2022). *Inequality kills: The unparalleled action needed to combat unprecedented inequality in the wake of COVID-19*. https://www.oxfam.org/en/research/inequality-kills

Parfit, D. (1984). *Reasons and persons*. Oxford University Press.

Participatory Budgeting Project. (2024). *History of PB*. https://www.participatorybudgeting.org

Participatory Grantmaking Community. (2023). *State of the movement*. https://www.participatorygrantmaking.org/

Participatory Grantmaking Community. (2024). *What is participatory grantmaking?* https://www.participatorygrantmaking.org/

Patagonia. (2022, September 14). *Earth is now our only shareholder.* https://www.patagonia.com/ownership/

PBNYC. (2024). *Participatory budgeting in New York City.* https://council.nyc.gov/pb

Peña-López, I., Barandiaran, X. E., & Calleja-López, A. (2020). *Decidim: The digital infrastructure for participatory democracy.* https://oidp.net/en/practice.php?id=1407

Pettit, P. (1997). *Republicanism: A theory of freedom and government.* Oxford University Press.

Pew Research Center. (2017). *Public trust in government: 1958–2017.* https://www.pewresearch.org/

Pew Research Center. (2021). *Public trust in government: 1958–2021.* https://www.pewresearch.org/

Pew Research Center. (2022). *Majorities of Americans say unions have a positive effect on U.S.* https://www.pewresearch.org/

Pew Research Center. (2023). *Public trust in government: 1958–2023.* https://www.pewresearch.org/

Pfeffer, F. T., & Killewald, A. (2018). Generations of advantage. Multigenerational correlations in family wealth. *Social Forces, 96*(4), 1411–1442.

Philanthropic Initiative for Racial Equity. (2019). *Grantmaking with a racial justice lens.* https://racialequity.org/

Piketty, T. (2014). *Capital in the twenty-first century* (A. Goldhammer, Trans.). Belknap Press.

Piketty, T., & Zucman, G. (2014). Capital is back: Wealth-income ratios in rich countries 1700–2010. *Quarterly Journal of Economics, 129*(3), 1255–1310.

Pontusson, J. (1987). *Radicalization and retreat: Swedish social democracy in the 1970s and 80s.* Cornell University Press.

Portuguese Government. (2024). *Orçamento participativo Portugal.* https://opp.gov.pt

Puppis, M., Valcke, P., & Sükösd, M. (2016). *Media ownership and concentration in Europe.*

Quillian, L., Pager, D., Hexel, O., & Midtbøen, A. H. (2017). Meta-analysis of field experiments shows no change in racial discrimination in hiring over time. *Proceedings of the National Academy of Sciences, 114*(41), 10870–10875.

Rawls, J. (1971). *A theory of justice*. Belknap Press.

Reardon, S. F. (2011). The widening academic achievement gap between the rich and the poor: New evidence and possible explanations. In G. J. Duncan & R. J. Murnane (Eds.), *Whither opportunity?* (pp. 91–116). Russell Sage Foundation.

Reckhow, S. (2013). *Follow the money: How foundation dollars change public school politics*. Oxford University Press.

Reckhow, S., & Snyder, J. W. (2014). The expanding role of philanthropy in education politics. *Educational Researcher, 43*(4), 186–195.

Reich, R. (2018). *Just giving: Why philanthropy is failing democracy and how it can do better*. Princeton University Press.

Repucci, S., & Slipowitz, A. (2021). *Democracy under siege. Freedom house special report*. https://freedomhouse.org/

Reuters/Ipsos. (2020). *Core political data*. https://www.ipsos.com/

Ribeiro, M. H., Ottoni, R., West, R., Almeida, V. A. F., & Meira, W. (2020). Auditing radicalization pathways on YouTube. In *Proceedings of the 2020 conference on fairness, accountability, and transparency* (pp. 131–141). Association for Computing Machinery, Inc.

Right Livelihood Foundation. (2024). *About the award*. https://rightlivelihood.org/

Roediger, D. R. (2007). *The wages of whiteness: Race and the making of the American working class*. Verso.

Rosenfeld, J. (2014). *What unions no longer do*. Harvard University Press.

Rothstein, R. (2004). *Class and schools: Using social, economic, and educational reform to close the Black-white achievement gap*. Teachers College Press.

Rothstein, R. (2017). *The color of law: A forgotten history of how our government segregated America*. Liveright.

Rowen, I. (2015). Inside Taiwan's sunflower movement: Twenty-four days in a student-occupied parliament and the future of the region. *Journal of Asian Studies, 74*(1), 5–21. https://doi.org/10.1017/S0021911814002174

Runciman, D. (2018). *How democracy ends*. Profile Books.

S&P 500 Index. (2024). *Market capitalization data*. Standard & Poor's.

Saez, E., & Zucman, G. (2019). *The triumph of injustice: How the rich dodge taxes and how to make them pay*. W. W. Norton & Company.

Sandel, M. J. (1996). *Democracy's discontent: America in search of a public philosophy*. Belknap Press.

Sanders, B. (2021). *For the 99.5% act: Summary*. Office of Senator Bernie Sanders.

Sanders, B., & Lee, B. (2021). *Tax on Wall Street Speculation Act*. U.S. Congress.

Scheffler, S. (2018). *Why worry about future generations?* Oxford University Press.

Scheiber, N., & Conger, K. (2020, November 4). *Uber and Lyft used a $200 million war chest to win in California*. The New York Times.

Scheppele, K. L. (2018). Autocratic legalism. *University of Chicago Law Review*, *85*(2), 545–583.

Schneider, J. (2015). *Beyond the schoolhouse gate*. Teachers College Press.

Schwab Foundation. (2020). *Social entrepreneurship report*. https://www.schwabfound.org/

Scott, M. (2021, June 15). *Seeding by ceding*. Medium.

Scott, M. (2024). *Yield giving*. https://yieldgiving.com

Sen, A. (1999). *Development as freedom*. Knopf.

Sentencing Project. (2022). *The color of justice: Racial and ethnic disparity in state prisons*. https://www.sentencingproject.org/

Seoul Metropolitan Government. (2024). *Participatory budgeting system*. https://english.seoul.go.kr/

Shapiro, T. M., Meschede, T., & Osoro, S. (2013). *The roots of the widening racial wealth gap: Explaining the black-white economic divide*. Institute on Assets and Social Policy.

Shearer, E. (2021). *Social media and news fact sheet*. Pew Research Center.

Shenker-Osorio, A. (2019). *Messaging this moment: A handbook for progressive communicators*. Center for Community Change.

Sherman Anti-Trust Act. (1890). *Congressional Record (Washington, Daily Edition), 21*, 2457. https://www.archives.gov/milestone-documents/sherman-anti-trust-act

Sierra Club. (2024). *Beyond coal: Outcomes*. https://coal.sierraclub.org

Sintomer, Y., Herzberg, C., & Röcke, A. (2013). *Participatory budgeting in Europe: Democracy and public governance*. Ashgate.

South African Reserve Bank. (2023). *Annual economic report*. https://www.resbank.co.za/

Storeng, K. T. (2014). The GAVI alliance and the 'Gates approach' to health system strengthening. *Global Public Health*, *9*(8), 865–879.

Strand, P. J. (2010). Inheriting inequality: Wealth, race, and the laws of succession. *Oregon Law Review*, *89*, 453.

Survey of Consumer Finances. (2024). *Wealth distribution*. Federal Reserve Board.

Tang, A. (2019). *Digital social innovation in Taiwan*. General resource for Digital Social Innovation. https://digitalsocial.eu/

Task Force on Climate-related Financial Disclosures. (2023). *2023 status report*. https://www.fsb-tcfd.org/

Tax Policy Center. (2024). *Key elements of the U.S. tax system: Estate tax*. Urban Institute & Brookings Institution.

Theoharis, J. (2018). *A more beautiful and terrible history: The uses and misuses of civil rights history*. Beacon Press.

UBS. (2025). *Global wealth report 2025*. https://www.ubs.com/global/en/family-office-uhnw/reports/global-wealth-report-2024.html

United Nations Fact-Finding Mission on Myanmar. (2018). *Report of the independent international fact-finding mission on Myanmar*. https://www.ohchr.org/en/hr-bodies/hrc/myanmar-ffm/index

Vieta, M. (2020). *Workers' buyouts: Cooperatives and the recovery of failing companies*. Pluto Press. https://www.plutobooks.com/

Ville de Paris. (2024). *Budget participatif: Bilan*. https://budgetparticipatif.paris.fr

Vogel, K. P. (2022, November 9). *Billionaire influence in the 2022 midterms*. The New York Times.

Vosoughi, S., Roy, D., & Aral, S. (2018). The spread of true and false news online. *Science, 359*(6380), 1146–1151.

Wampler, B. (2007). *Participatory budgeting in Brazil: Contestation, cooperation, and accountability*. Pennsylvania State University Press.

Wampler, B. (2019). *Participatory budgeting: Spreading across the globe*. Cambridge University Press. https://www.cambridge.org/

Wampler, B., McNulty, S. L., & Touchton, M. (2019). *Democracy at work in an unequal world: Participatory budgeting in civil society*. Cambridge University Press.

Warren, E. (2018). *Accountable capitalism act*. U.S. Senate.

Warren, E. (2020). *Plans: Ultra-millionaire tax*. Elizabeth Warren for President.

West Health-Gallup. (2021). *The 2021 healthcare in America report*. https://www.westhealth.org/

Western, B. (2018). *Homeward: Life in the year after prison*. Russell Sage Foundation.

White House. (2024). *Budget of the U.S. Government: Fiscal year 2025*. https://www.whitehouse.gov/omb/budget/

Wilson, V., & Rodgers, W. M., III (2016). *Black-white wage gaps expand with rising wage inequality*. Economic Policy Institute.

Winters, J. A. (2011). *Oligarchy*. Cambridge University Press.

World Health Organization. (2023). *World malaria report 2023*. https://www.who.int/

World Meteorological Organization. (2024). *State of the global climate 2023*. https://wmo.int/

World Values Survey. (2023). *WVS wave 7 (2017–2022)*. https://www.worldvaluessurvey.org/

WWF. (2022). *Living planet report 2022*. https://livingplanet.panda.org/

Zamagni, S., & Zamagni, V. (2010). *Cooperative enterprise: Facing the challenge of globalization*. Edward Elgar.

INDEX

Printed and bound by CPI Group (UK) Ltd, Croydon, CR0 4YY

28/05/2026

14889158-0002